Praise for

THE FACE OF ADDICTION

"There's only one solid way to make change in a social problem—hear the stories of the folks involved. Their authentic voices, the poignant twists in their lives let us know that we walk with them and they with us. This is true of the addiction epidemic that plagues America, and *The Face of Addiction* brings them out of the shadows in powerful ways and make this book essential reading for us all."

– Sam Quinones
Author of *Dreamland: The True Tale of America's Opiate Epidemic*

"Empathetic, honest, and humanizing. Joshua Lawson's heart-wrenching book *The Face of Addiction, a* collection of first-hand accounts of addiction in Appalachian Ohio, is defiant and life-affirming. He pushes against traditional narratives with love and grace. Lawson teaches readers to listen with open hearts and in so doing reveals a way forward, a path towards addressing stigma and the underlying causes of addiction."

– Jack Shuler
Author of *This is Ohio: The Overdose Crisis and the Front Lines of a New America*

"*The Face of Addiction* offers tremendous insight into substance use and addiction through the voluntary stories of people with lived experience, and those who have been directly affected. Rarely does the public get to hear such personal and poignantly told stories by the very people most affected by the current addiction and mental health crisis. The author provides a rare opportunity to witness the struggles, strengths, failures, and successes of people who are often overlooked, as we as a nation attempt to address these issues. Compassionate and inspiring, readers are left with a better understanding of these issues, and how we as a society have, in many ways, contributed to them."

– Lisa Roberts
R.N./Public Health Nurse, Portsmouth City Health Department

"I have been grateful to know Joshua Lawson as a pastor, activist, and friend for several years. Now with *The Face of Addiction*, I'm getting to know him as a writer, and I'm inspired. He presents a series of vulnerable and hopeful vignettes that harmonize with one message: people who use drugs are beloved by God. Lawson's faith and relationships compel him to resist the deadly stigma and shame that harms people who use drugs and instead see the face, the person, the child of God behind the veil of addiction, incarceration, and chaos. For both veterans of the recovery or harm reduction communities, as well as folks exploring the complexities of substance use disorder for the first time, *The Face of Addiction* is an invaluable resource.

– **Rev. Dan Clark**
Ohio Director, Faith in Public Life

"*The Face of Addiction* offers a powerful look at substance use disorder from multiple perspectives by highlighting how addiction impacts everyone in its path. It is storytelling at its best, the kind that creates a deep empathy in the reader for the raw, moment-to-moment struggle to find hope and recovery. Lawson's profound reflections, based on the lived experiences of the people he interviewed for this book, will challenge your underlying beliefs about addiction and jolt you out of compassion fatigue. He obliterates the stigma and shame by humanizing the struggle of addiction in a way that will induce true cultural change. Furthermore, Lawson compassionately delivers the raw truth about the gaps that exist between the multiple valid paths to recovery. *The Face of Addiction* is a must read for all of us who have the courage to seek understanding, change, and hope for those who struggle with addiction."

– **Kendra Cram**
Social Emotional Learning Teacher, Minford, Ohio

"First, I should confess that I don't consider myself a good example of faith-in-action, which might be the only genuine kind of faith. Those of us who can manage to get by without much of it generally do. However, we often fool ourselves by mislabeling things that keep us from needing or acting upon genuine faith as faith. The courageous volunteers who share their stories in *The Face of Addiction* do not have that luxury. To survive their hardships and have a chance at a decent and fulfilling life, they have been forced to act upon a faith that believes something better is possible for them. They may not call it "faith," but what else could it be when their own experience and most of society says that what they have achieved, namely recovery, is not possible? Lawson seems to recognize how much our world needs this type of faith-in-action to take hold beyond just those of us who are most desperate for change. It is clear that he is moved and inspired by the people he interviewed and wishes to share that experience with the world. Even more than that, he encourages us to find our own first hand inspiration by looking to those we might be inclined to write off rather than learn from, suggesting that in doing so we might both help each other find what we're looking for."

– Chad Royer
PharmD, JD, CSPI Drug and Poison Information Center, Cincinnati's Children's Hospital Medical Center

"I grew up as an AA kid with a Dad who was a recovering alcoholic and prescription drug abuser. I also lived in Appalachia for four years, where I observed firsthand the impact of the opioid crisis on my neighbors and friends. And I currently work for a non-profit where addiction is a reality for many of the people we serve. I can say unequivocally that Joshua Lawson accomplished his goal in writing *The Face of Addiction*. It reveals the diverse backgrounds and stories of a frequently stereotyped group of people. Too many times I've heard the phrase "those people" used in reference to people who use drugs. Lawson reminds us that "those people" have a story not at all unlike our own. Stories of love, family, heartache, trauma, and pain. And through these stories, he reignites the hope that recovery and healing are possible. "Those people" have a face. In fact, they have many faces. I hope you are as impacted as I was as you take the time to read this book and gaze upon them. Because I believe you will discover that the face you're looking at resembles your daughter, your son, your spouse, your neighbor, and perhaps even your own."

– Andrew Wehrheim
Inventory Coordinator, The Hope Center

"Joshua is a storyteller and it shows in his work, *The Face of Addiction*. He has collected a series of true stories about the people that are so often disregarded, overlooked and shunned in our society. This book gives a real and human account of what addiction looks like in Appalachia and it isn't what you have seen on the news. Joshua breaks the typical stigma that is associated with addiction in Appalachia and instead receives these powerful stories and anchors them in hope. It is clear that Joshua's conviction—that every person has the potential to change the world—is the driving force behind his work. *The Face of Addiction* is a testimony to this belief."

– Rev. Paul Bennett
All Saints Episcopal Church

"In *The Face of Addiction*, Joshua Lawson takes us behind the politics and headlines to offer a glimpse at the very human cost of both drug addiction and the war on drugs. As a family member of someone suffering from Substance Use Disorder, I thought I was well engaged on this issue. This book opened my eyes to exactly how apathetic I had become to the very real human suffering all around us. More than that, the book provides practical steps for all of us who are ready to more thoughtfully engage the people and policies behind the pain."

– Jason Elam
Host of The Messy Spirituality Podcast

"Southern Ohio has long been represented as the face of addiction in rural America, often being labeled as the "Pill Mill Capital" of the United States and ground zero for the opioid crisis. Many people have come to the area to paint a very superficial picture of what those labels truly mean, however. In *The Face of Addiction*, Joshua Lawson transforms that nebulous image into something profoundly personal. With great care, he provides a platform for the human stories that often get lost among the national headlines, allowing space for vulnerability and honesty without exploiting or sensationalizing the people whose stories he shares. If you want to understand how southern Ohio has changed, and how our families, friends, and communities have lived, mourned, rallied, and recovered through this crisis, then read Joshua's book."

– Abby Spears
Harm Reductionist & Community Organizer with River Valley Organizing
and the Scioto County Collaborative Opioid Consortium

*Stories
of Loss and
Recovery*

THE
FACE
OF
ADDICTION

JOSHUA LAWSON

Cover design and layout by Rafael Polendo (polendo.net)
Cover image by nevodka (shutterstock.com)

First Edition

ISBN 978-1-938480-90-4

This volume is printed on acid free paper and meets ANSI Z39.48 standards.

Printed in the United States of America

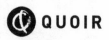 QUOIR

Published by Quoir
Oak Glen, California
www.quoir.com

DEDICATED

To the people whose stories are contained in these pages. You are some of the bravest souls with whom I've ever been privileged to work. The fact that you trusted me to share your stories with the world is one of the greatest honors I will ever receive.

CONTENTS

PREFACE

Let's pretend we have a time machine and that you've travelled back with me about four years. You see that guy over there in the corner with the salt-and-pepper hair and a downcast look on his face, the one who appears to be at his wits end? Yeah, that's the one. Well, that guy is me. I'm lost, lonely, and confused—or at least, I was—trapped in the most desperate experience of my life.

Long before I ever got involved in recovery work or had the idea to write this book, I was struggling (and failing) to navigate a relationship with someone close to me that had become very dysfunctional. The details of that situation are better left unspoken, but trust me when I say that it was the most painful experience of my life. No matter how hard I tried, I just couldn't solve the problem. As a result, my physical health was deteriorating and I was becoming depressed. The situation had gone so far off the rails that it was even beginning to threaten the well-being of my family.

It was precisely at that point when I realized that something had to give. So, I sought counseling. I read books. I shared my struggle with a few trusted friends. Desperate for relief, I even tried bypassing the pain altogether by "giving it to God" in prayer. Nothing seemed to help. Finally, all my resources were exhausted and I hit my own personal rock bottom.

That's when two men crossed my path and changed the course of my life forever. One of them was a friend of a friend who reached out to me after seeing one of my social media posts online. He lives two hours away, but he brought his boat down and took me out on the river to just hang out and talk about life. In the years that have passed since our first meeting, we've only missed getting together once a month a few times, most of them due to the coronavirus pandemic.

The other guy was an artist whose music I just happened to encounter on the radio on my drive to work one morning. His band has been around for a while but I'd never heard of them before. The raw emotional content of their lyrics arrested my attention, resonating deeply in my heart. All the light and darkness of the lead singer's personal journey reflected beautifully in the band's musical evolution.

These details may not interest you, but the point is that those guys saved my life. The first through his friendship and the second through his art. Where other people, even professionals, had failed to reach me at my point of need, those guys succeeded in giving me the tools I required to find a clear path through my relational mess.

Now, this is more than just a touching story. The plot twist here is that both those men are in active recovery from substance use disorder. If you asked them, they would gladly tell you all about the personal challenges they have faced related to their past drug use. Depression. Anxiety. Broken relationships. Suicidal ideations. You name it. But somehow, they emerged from the abyss of their dark ordeal onto the path of healing and wholeness. And they brought the "treasures of darkness" with them—the kind of insight that could help a guy like me face down his own inner demons.

This interesting correlation didn't occur to me until a few years later when I was campaigning for criminal justice reform in the state of Ohio, trying to shift the public narrative concerning people who use drugs. In the process of advocating for a more compassionate approach to addiction, I had started getting close to folks who were suffering the full weight of the opioid crisis. The more I listened to the tales of their struggle, the better I understood the nature of addiction.

As I tried to articulate this growing insight to other people, they would sometimes ask me why I cared so much about the issue since I had never experienced drug addiction myself. And that's when it dawned on me. Maybe my advocacy was a way of paying forward the help I'd received from those two guys. After all, they were the kind of men whom society will often write off as "junkies," "addicts," or "users." Some people will even go so far as to argue that their lives are worthless and not worth preserving.

But how could I ever accept such stigma, having seen the incredible value that those two "junkies" brought to my life at a time when no one else, myself included, was able to do the trick? They reached me at my lowest point when no one else could. They literally changed the course of my life forever. And they did it by speaking to me out of their own painful experience with substance use disorder.

I wrote this book for people like them—for anyone who has ever gotten lost in the dark woods of drug addiction. My dedication to this work is fueled by the simple conviction that there's not a single person out there with a needle in their arm right now who doesn't have the potential to change the world. People who use drugs are loved by God, they belong in our communities, and their lives are full of meaning.

Furthermore, those who struggle with addiction have been graced with a unique insight into the human condition that we would be foolish to dismiss. Sure, they may have chosen unhealthy ways to cope with their pain, but who hasn't? Honestly, I've lost all patience for people who look down their noses at those who use drugs just because their own poor coping mechanisms are more socially acceptable. Recovery is hard enough on its own. Those who struggle under the weight of addiction don't need the further impediment of social stigma blocking their way to healing.

I'm just a normie, so I only know so much, but what I do know is that people who have fallen prey to the specter of substance use disorder—for *whatever* reason—deserve our compassion. They deserve friends and allies who will fight for them to have easy access to treatment and all the harm reduction services they need to stay alive, in the hope that one day they will get back on their feet and enjoy their lives to the fullest.

With any luck, *The Face of Addiction* will help break down the stigma against people who use drugs that still pervades American culture. Because even as my own story shows, as much as our friends and family who struggle with addiction need our help, we need theirs just as much.

CANARIES IN A COAL MINE: A BRIEF HISTORY OF THE OPIOID CRISIS IN SOUTHERN OHIO

Opioid prescription painkillers are a class of drugs considered controlled substances based on a classification system initiated by the U.S. Drug Enforcement Administration (DEA). The Controlled Substances Act (CSA) places substances with accepted medical uses into one of four schedules, with the substances with the highest potential for harm and abuse being placed in Schedule II, and substances with progressively less potential for harm and abuse being placed in Schedules III through V.

Opioids, also considered narcotics "from the Greek word for 'stupor,'" originally referred to "a variety of substances that dulled the senses and relieved pain" (Drug Enforcement Agency, n.d.). Opioid prescription painkillers are commonly used for managing pain. In the mid 1990's, major changes occurred in the United States in the way that these controlled substances were prescribed—primarily relating to a new movement to treat pain more aggressively in the community setting. The pharmaceutical industry responded with the creation of new potent opioid painkillers, many of which went on to become "blockbuster drugs." They generated billions of dollars in revenue for their parent companies, and, increasingly companies began to make more powerful opioid painkillers. The risk of addiction was downplayed significantly as prescriptions soared.

Reports of prescription drug abuse in southern Ohio and throughout the Appalachian region first began to appear in reports and the national media around the year 2000. These reports primarily mentioned the new potent painkiller OxyContin, although other pain pills such as hydrocodone-based products were already well established. OxyContin is a brand name prescription painkiller that contains the opioid oxycodone. What made it different than other "common" opioids at that time was its sheer potency as a pure oxycodone product packed into a time-release pill that could easily be crushed to release the medication "all at once" producing a euphoric feeling similar to heroin. One report stated that between March 11, 2000 and March 31, 2003 there were 573 stories in major U.S. papers which mentioned OxyContin in their title or lead paragraph. One of the earliest stories related to OxyContin to be featured in a major national publication was in U.S. News & World Report in February 2001 entitled "The Poor Man's Heroin" based on a Scioto County, Ohio physician who had been indicted for providing illegitimate prescriptions for OxyContin for cash. The article described Dr. John Lilly who practiced medicine like a common drug dealer. Dr. Lilly was eventually arrested for flagrantly trading OxyContin prescriptions in exchange for "stolen" automatic weapons to two undercover police officers and FBI agents. In 2000 Portsmouth—Scioto County's seat—first began to see an increase in fatal overdoses, crime, and opioid addiction related to OxyContin. Pharmacy and bank robberies also rose as more desperate and addicted people began to commit crimes to feed their addictions. It was the beginning of a long decade of human and social fallout from overprescribing prescription opioids.

In 2001, an article in The Guardian described the proliferation of OxyContin in the Appalachian region, even dubbing it "hillbilly heroin" due to its popularity throughout the mountainous regions of Appalachia (Borger, 2001). Over the next few years, many major publications such as Time, Newsweek, and the New York Times featured reports on the prescription pain pill epidemic exploding throughout Appalachia. They described stories of small rural areas that were being destroyed by pain killers such as OxyContin.

In 2000, the Appalachian Region was categorized as having the highest rates of OxyContin prescriptions per capita, according to an IMS Health and National Prescription Audit Plus Evaluation. Widespread abuse of the drug was prevalent as was diversion for profit in a growing practice referred to by law enforcement as "pill dealing". Portsmouth, Ohio, became a hotspot for illegitimate pain clinics from 2000-2011, and thus for spreading of prescriptions across southern Ohio and Appalachia.

In 2007, one high-profile pain clinic in Portsmouth was raided by the Drug Enforcement Agency (DEA). Dr. Paul Volkman, identified by the DEA as "the largest physician dispenser of oxycodone in the U.S. from 2003–2005," was eventually convicted and sentenced to four consecutive life sentences for his role in the illegal distribution of prescription drugs (Martin, 2011). But by 2010, Scioto County, Ohio, had half-a-dozen additional illegitimate pain clinics becoming a main distribution point for controlled substances in the region. The opioid distribution rate was 123 individual pain pills per citizen—by far the highest in the state of Ohio. Additionally, Scioto County's fatal overdose rate was nearly triple the state average, and one in ten newborns experienced days of opioid withdrawal after birth leading to medical and social problems for these infants.

In January 2010, Scioto County became the first county in the nation to declare a public health emergency. In 2011, Ohio changed state laws to regulate pain management clinics, and the DEA eventually indicted numerous physicians and clinic owners from Scioto County. However, Florida became the national epicenter of illegitimate pain clinics. Carloads of local addicted citizens made regular trips south to score pain pills then transport them back to southern Ohio for illegal distribution.

Opioid pain medication and heroin are nearly identical in chemical structure. The overprescribing of prescription opioids created an enormous swath of people who are chemically dependent on opioids. Prescription opioids became much more difficult to get—but opioid addiction is a chronic condition. Beginning in 2011, southern Ohio experienced a rapid influx of heroin and illicitly manufactured analog opioids that continues to this day. As pain pills have become more regulated thus scarcer, heroin has infiltrated the Appalachian region leading to brand new problems and social fallout in a region that was previously of little interest to major drug cartels and metropolitan gangs.

Whereas the Appalachian region had struggled with the prescription drug and painkiller problem since around the year 2000, the rest of the nation was not as affected. Beginning around 2010, the problem spread across the country and attracted more state and federal attention. According to the Centers for Disease Control (CDC), between 1999 and 2017, almost 218,000 people died in the United States from overdoses related to prescription opioids. Overdose deaths involving prescription opioids were five times higher in 2017 than in 1999 (Centers for Disease Control and Prevention, n.d.).

In October of 2017, the United States President directed the Department of Health and Human Services to declare the opioid crisis a national public health emergency. The epidemic continues to ravage most parts of the nation. The most recent complete data from the Ohio Department of Health and Centers for Disease Control shows Ohio ranked as one of the top five states with the most fatal overdose rates in the nation with 3,980 in 2018 alone. The nearly complete death data from 2019 shows that Ohio dropped slightly to 3,957 overdose deaths while Scioto County recorded a record 80 deaths—an 18% increase over the previous year, which gives the county the highest death rate of any county in Ohio's history (Ohio Department of Health, 2019). The increased presence of deadly analog fentanyl drugs into the illicit opioid supply is now largely responsible for overdose deaths. Southern Ohio residents were indeed the "canaries in the coal mine" in terms of recognizing the devastating impact of opioid misuse and addiction.

– **Lisa Roberts R.N.**
Portsmouth City Health Department

"I UNDERSTAND THIS BETTER NOW."

In the summer of 2009 in the heart of southern Ohio, the prescription pain pill epidemic was escalating. Doctors were handing out scripts for Percocet, Vicodin, Morphine, and other medicines like they were candy. People were in pain, in need of help, end of story. At least, that was the narrative many of the pharmaceutical companies were pushing on doctors. In reality, it was just the beginning of the story.

I remember that year vividly. I had a cavity in the back of my mouth pressing on an overgrown wisdom tooth. As you can imagine, the stabbing sensations I felt were a daily reminder that I had spent too many years drinking Mountain Dew. Suffice it to say, I learned my lesson and gave up the hard, sugary stuff that summer.

However, extracting a wisdom tooth and filling a cavity is not a simple matter when you're uninsured. My wife and I had two kids at the time. I was making just ten dollars an hour as a landscape laborer on an irregular schedule. One "rainy day" was enough to set us back for the month. We couldn't easily afford such luxuries as health insurance, so there I was, literally aching for relief until we could pay for the necessary dental work. So, I suffered through it for a while. I did my best to manage the pain, but sometimes it got so bad I couldn't focus on my work. Intervention arrived when my dad offered to share his painkillers.

Dad wasn't a recreational drug user, not by a long shot, but he did have cancer, a really nasty kind that gave him a lot of pain, especially during treatments. Consequently, he had nearly unlimited access to pain medication. He only took these pills when necessary, though. Dad was a beast of a man who preferred to live with his pain if he could rather than try to relieve it with chemical substances, so he was happy to share a few with me if he thought they would help.

And they did, somewhat. I've always had a high tolerance for medication, and tooth pain is some of the worst there is, so on my most sensitive days, I really had to pop the pills to put those nerve endings to sleep. It didn't take long for me to realize two things: 1) too many opiates can really "bind you up" as my grandmother used to say. In other words, the constipation sucks; and 2) taking opiates feels good.

I never crushed and snorted a pill or pushed anything into my veins, so I can't comment on the euphoric rush; however, consuming just a few pills was enough to give me a soothing feeling of underlying calm. That's what I remember most about the experience. And to be honest, there were some days when I didn't actually need to take them, but I did. Technically, I guess that's enough to qualify for abuse, or at least misuse.

Fortunately, my experience with pain pills went no further than that. I eventually saved up enough cash, got my wisdom tooth yanked, and filled that nagging cavity. Problem solved. Dad quit offering me pills and I didn't ask for anymore. Yet, I'd be lying if I said the thought never crossed my mind. That's how much I liked the feeling. Not only did I enjoy the calming effect of opiates, but I also saw how useful they could be in dealing with anxiety and certain stressful situations.

You might be nodding your head in agreement as you read these words. I wish I could say that I didn't know so many people whose experience with opioid use began innocently enough, like mine, but then went on to destroy their lives whereas mine simply ended. Most folks started with a legitimate prescription but then spiraled into uncontrollable substance use disorder. Some of them died from that abuse, either through overdose or other health-related complications, while many others are still trapped in the merciless cycle of addiction as we speak. Others live in recovery with a long road of suffering behind them.

Take my friend, "Eric," for instance. Eric and I went to the same high school back in the early 2000s. We played basketball and ran around together all the time. He was one of my closest friends. Life took us in different directions after high school, but we always remained in touch. One day, Eric hurt his back while playing ball. A doctor gave him a prescription to manage the pain. The rest, as they say, is history.

I saw Eric a couple times in 2006 after I moved back home from college. He was married to his high school sweetheart. They owned their own home and were awaiting the arrival of their first child. Then, we lost contact. I heard some gossip about his condition, but I didn't make any effort to follow up. The next time I saw him was on my front porch in 2009. He came by asking for gas money to help one of his family members get their "meds" from a doctor in West Virginia.

I knew Eric was lying to me, but I couldn't bring myself to confront him. I just didn't get it. I looked at him, unsure of what to say. He was visibly nervous, shaking somewhat and pacing back and forth. I questioned the details of his story and tried to give him every opportunity to tell me the truth, but he persisted. He left me standing on the porch that day without a shred of real understanding.

How could he stand here and lie right to my face after all we've been through? I wondered. *Doesn't our friendship mean anything?*

Of course, it did. Eric didn't mean to hurt me. At least, that wasn't his intention. He was the same guy I knew through high school and that guy was undoubtedly good. He wasn't a criminal, but he also wasn't himself. In that moment, the addiction had control of him. He saw an opportunity to exploit my kindness—that was all. The long-term effect of his actions wasn't on his mind. All he knew was that he needed a fix. I understand this better now.

That's how it went for a lot of people during the early days of the opioid crisis in central Appalachia. That's how it could have went for me, too. What made the difference? I'll never know for sure. All I know is that it took nearly a decade before I would start to get close to an answer.

"THERE'S ONLY ONE WAY TO DEAL WITH AN ADDICT: A TALL TREE AND A SHORT ROPE."

In his 2015 book, *Just Mercy*, attorney Bryan Stevenson tells a story about his grandmother that helped direct his journey toward the work of social justice. Growing up amidst racial bigotry in southern America, he recalls her always saying, "You can't understand most of the important things from a distance, Bryan. You have to get close."

Aside from his work as a law professor at New York University Law School, Stevenson is the executive director of the Equal Justice Initiative in Montgomery, Alabama. His advocacy has won relief for multiple victims of systemic injustice within America's prison system. I read Stevenson's book for the first time during the summer of 2018, shortly after I quit my job as a mail carrier for the United States Postal Service. Despite the fantastic pay and benefits that came with being a federal employee, I found myself longing to move toward a more fulfilling vocation, something that would allow me to pursue my personal interests while utilizing my gifts for the benefit of other people.

One day, a professor friend of mine from our local university sent me a job posting from an organization called Faith in Public Life. The mid-term elections were just getting ready to fire up across the state of Ohio, and there was a constitutional amendment some people were trying to get on the ballot dealing with issues of drug treatment and criminal justice reform. Faith in Public Life had received funding to expand their work, which was normally more urban-focused, into the southernmost reaches of the state. Rural Appalachia. My neck of the woods.

So, I applied. When the call finally came for an interview, I sold myself like it was nobody's business. As fate would have it, I got the job. Thus began my first formal experience as a community organizer.

Many memories from that season stand out to me now. I wouldn't trade the relationships and perspectives I gained from the work for anything. Although the campaign itself ended in overwhelming defeat—we knew it would be an uphill battle from the get-go, but we were still deflated when the final numbers came rolling in—my engagement in that effort opened other doors for me to be involved in my community and even provided the kernel of inspiration for writing this book. It gave me the time and resources I needed to "get close" to the people who were most directly affected by the opioid crisis. Everything I have learned from then until now has proven to me the truth of Stevenson's grandmother's words. Important things cannot be understood from a distance.

Early in the campaign, I got an emergency call to travel to a small town in Noble County, Ohio, to help collect the remaining signatures that were needed to get the proposed amendment on the ballot before the deadline. I never realized before, but it takes an insane amount of work just to bring an issue to vote in a statewide election. I had never been to this town, but I had seen many like it. Wedged in a small valley between the hills, it struck me as the kind of place you'd imagine from a Stephen King novel, where everything is normal and nice among the sleepy townspeople until, of course, it isn't. Our rag-tag canvassing team met up at a local diner, the name of which I have long since forgotten. After lunch, we split into pairs and divvied up the surrounding neighborhoods for door-knocking duties—my least favorite thing in the whole world to do.

My pitch went something like this: "Hello. My name is Josh. I'm collecting signatures to get an issue on the ballot where people can vote to direct more of our public funds to drug treatment instead of prison for people who suffer with addiction. Would you like to see this issue on the ballot?"

Most of the people we talked to were nice enough, even the ones who politely said, "Thanks, but no thanks." But in certain instances, we encountered some pretty clear prejudices. Like the guy who said we'd be better off trying to protect honeybees than helping "those people." While I'm all for protecting the honeybees, both then and now, I wondered what relevance that dichotomy was supposed to have for the conversation about providing better access to drug treatment.

That response was fairly benign compared to others we ran into, though, both in Noble County and other parts of the state. At one public meeting, a sheriff in central Ohio said, "There's only one way to deal with an addict: a tall tree and a short rope." At another venue, the local sheriff shared his conviction that the public response to drug use should be to replace whatever substance people had in their syringes with cyanide. Yes, cyanide.

These were publicly elected officials, by the way. Beyond their few examples, I couldn't begin to name the many first responders, police officers, and fire fighters around the state and country who have spoken out in public or posted similar sentiments on their social media pages.

Back home, I spent a lot of time talking one-on-one with local community leaders about issues related to drug addiction and how we respond to addicted people in our society. Early in the campaign,

I sought to immunize them from the inevitable onslaught of propaganda that I knew would come out once the issue became public.

"It's important that we understand what's really going on here," I said, "because this is an issue that the general public will be easily swayed over with a billboard that says something stupid like, 'Vote no on Issue 1! Keep the criminals behind bars where they belong!'"

Without fail, the person I was talking to would laugh and nod their head in agreement. However, many of them ghosted me later on. Often, they were either unable or simply too afraid to take a clear stand on the kind of criminal justice reform that they initially agreed the state needed to pursue. Imagine the irony I felt about a month before Election Day when, while driving through Portsmouth, I came across a large trailer sitting in a vacant lot at a busy intersection. The brightly-colored banner hung securely from its side read, "Keep criminals and drug dealers off our streets! Vote NO on Issue 1."

I relate these stories simply to give you a general feel for the social climate surrounding drug addiction that pervades Appalachian culture. When it comes to substance use disorder, the struggle and the shame is real, no doubt, but so is the stigma. In fact, I can only imagine how the shame that keeps so many people trapped in the dark room of addiction is compounded by such displays of social ignorance.

There is a dark and foreboding relationship between shame and stigma, after all. Any battle is far more difficult to win when the lines have been drawn on two separate fronts, and the barriers to healing from the pain associated with substance use disorder are both personal and social. The twin experience of these two monsters lies somewhere near the heart of every individual's experience of addiction. Taken together, they create a formidable obstacle to recovery.

Shame is that beast which lurks in the shadows of the human psyche, feeding on feelings of unworthiness and helplessness. We all deal with it to a certain degree as part of the general human condition, but people with addiction experience shame as a special kind of hell, one in which they feel hopelessly lost and often despair of finding any safe passage out of. Desperately feeling their way around in hopes of an exit, they happen upon a door only to find it barred shut. Stigma stands guard like a sentinel on the outside, strengthening the power and presence of shame within. This matters to people seeking recovery because according to Dr. Brené Brown, a researcher and best-selling author at the University Of Houston Graduate College Of Social Work, "Shame corrodes the very part of us that believes we are capable of change" (Brown, 2007).

And what about stigma? Merriam-Webster defines it as "a mark of shame or discredit." It is borrowed from a Latin word which means "mark" or "brand" and ultimately derives from the Greek word *stizein*, meaning "to tattoo." The earliest English use of the word *stigma* referred to a scar left by a hot iron. This idea of scarring or branding has carried over into the popular modern use of the word which most often refers to "a set of negative and often unfair beliefs that a society or group of people have about something" ("Stigma," n.d.).

Of course, it is easy to see how stigma both produces and reinforces the stories we tell ourselves in society about certain groups of people—in this case, about people who use drugs. Challenging these cultural narratives is important because they unconsciously dictate many things about our society, such as how we feel about our neighbors, how we vote on important issues, and how we prioritize public funding.

Overcoming the stigma surrounding drug addiction is no small feat, but I am convinced that the most effective way to do so is by telling the stories of people who use drugs and those who love them from a new perspective—humanizing rather than dehumanizing their struggle. This is what I've tried to do in the following chapters. I've sought to center the lived experience of twelve courageous souls who were brave enough to trust me with their stories. I offer their insight to you now with the hope that you will see what I have seen in each one of them—though scarred, the overwhelmingly beautiful face of addiction.

"HE TRIED SO HARD TO STAY AWAY FROM IT."

Joe Runyon was a legend. Just ask any of his friends. Or better yet, ask his wife, Laurie. Ask her about Joe's arm bands, his studded belt, or the knee-high moccasins he always liked to wear. She'll laugh out loud, and her eyes will light up with a hundred stories that tell you all you need to know about her feelings for Joe.

Every smile is tinged with sadness, though, because on the evening of October 31, 2018, Laurie awoke to find Joe laying on their kitchen floor. The sight was unbelievable at first. Joe had been clean since April and drugs were the furthest thing from Laurie's mind. But the needle in his hand told her everything she didn't want to hear. Laurie had been looking forward to visiting her sister in Alaska with Joe the next summer. As fate would have it, she ended up sprinkling Joe's ashes over the ocean instead.

I met with Laurie at the Lofts Coffee Shop in Portsmouth in early December 2018, just a few months after Joe's passing. She laughed a lot during our time together. She cried some, too. I was honored to bear witness to both her joy and her grief as she shared her most cherished memories of Joe.

This is their story.

⊖ ⊖ ⊖

On the 500 block of Chillicothe Street in Portsmouth sits a little bar called Frankenstein's. Laurie met Joe at Frankenstein's one evening in 1987 during his "clean" years.

"This is kind of funny," Laurie says. "I was out with a guy who I was dating and Joe was out with a married woman. We just started talking. Me and the guy I was with actually had a big fight that night because he said, 'I know you like him!' I replied, 'I just met him, how do I know if I like him? Just because we were smiling in the same direction ... '"

She grins.

"Oh, but what can I say about Joe? He was just so vivacious. Music was his thing. It seems like everything we did together revolved around music. He would listen to music from the time he went to bed all night long. He'd just leave the T.V. on with music playing. And it seems like everywhere we went, we always ran into someone Joe knew. That's just the kind of guy he was. It didn't matter who you were either—rich or poor, whatever—he treated everyone the same. He had a good heart.

"He was a hard worker, too, and he was always proud of that. He started working when he was thirteen years old. Of course, he did a lot of drugs when he was younger. He almost got caught selling cocaine once. He had a bunch of it on him and the officer asked if he had a problem. Joe said, 'No, I don't,' and he never touched it again— for twenty years, at least. That's when we met, during his 'clean' years. At first we were just friends. He actually tried to get me to fix him up with my best friend, but I said, 'She's not gonna go out with you, you're too wild.' So, I asked him out instead. He came home with me that night and never left. That was 1990, three years after we first met.

"We rented a house in Rosemount on the Eden Park side. We had all kinds of parties and stuff at that house. His brother would come over a lot and we would drink, but nothing else. We did all kinds of thing together. We got married in '92 with a big wedding and a thing at the house afterwards. Joe was working at Mill's Pride then. He started off temporary but worked his way up to supervisor. Then he worked at a few other places before getting a job at the Coke plant, where he stayed until they closed down in 2002. After that, he went back to school at the vo-tech [vocational-technical school]. That's when he started on the crack.

"He always said, 'I never thought it would get me', you know, because he'd done all that other stuff before and was able to walk away. The first time I found out about it, though, was after Thanksgiving that year. I was missing money, like $800. At first, he tried to act like he didn't know anything about it, but then he called me back at work and said, 'I need to tell you something.' When he told me, I said, 'You've got to be kidding me.' I was shocked.

"But he tried, he really did. He tried so hard to stay away from it. When he went around certain people, though, it's like he couldn't resist. His friend would call, and he'd go off again. I got so angry with this one friend of his. He got arrested one time, and I said, 'I hope they bury you under the jail!' I know that's not nice, but I was angry."

Laurie looks at the floor and sighs.

"There were just so many ups and downs with Joe. I'd get mad, I would cry, I'd beg him to stay home ... It took him five years to get off the crack. And he wouldn't have got off, I think, if he hadn't got caught breaking into pop machines. You know, he said he wasn't actually doing it; he was just driving the car, but I told him, 'Either way, you're gonna go to jail over it.' There were two guys breaking into the machines for change, and he was driving the truck. Of course, when they got caught, all the stuff was in his car, so ...

"He would always say, 'I think I'll get over it. Maybe it's just a phase I'm going through.' I said, 'No, Joe, I don't think this is a phase. I think you need help.' But he always thought he could beat it. Eventually, we got him into a rehab up in Huntington. They put him in detox for three days, but then the insurance wouldn't cover anything else. So we took him to Dayton to the Salvation Army thing which didn't cost anything. He was supposed to stay there for six months, but he only stayed forty days." Laurie shakes her head. "We ended up having to file bankruptcy because we thought we were gonna lose our house.

"I couldn't tell you how many cars we went through. I went to the guys Joe worked with and told them, 'Guys, quit giving him money. I've got bills to pay, so if you give him money, you're not gonna get it back.' So the dealers told him he could drive for them to pay for his drugs instead. The first time he disappeared, he was gone for like a week. Everybody we knew was trying to find him. Finally, I found him in Rosemount in the Big Bear parking lot. He'd been high for seven days, and he looked *awful*. He hadn't eaten or anything. I took him to McDonald's to get him something to eat and he could not even function. He couldn't hold the fork to eat. It was just unreal."

Laurie's voice strains at this point as if she can't even believe what's she's saying.

"Well, once he finally got straight again, he went back to working construction. It's funny because Joe always worked when he was off the stuff. One day, though, I got a call from someone who said they saw our car down at the Royal Motel. I thought, 'Oh, you've got to be kidding me. Not again.' So, I went down there and made a terrible scene. I was screaming at the top of my lungs, saying, 'Joe F-n Runyon, get your ass out here!' He wouldn't come out, and they wouldn't tell me which room he was in either. I ended up calling the cops. I was gonna have him arrested, but they told me I couldn't do that because we were married. They did tell me I could have the car towed, though, so that's what I did, and Joe got beat up because of it.

"I don't know, though," she says, looking down again as if she's trying to make sense of it all. "He would do really good for six months, and then he'd be gone again. It was almost always when his friend would call. I told Joe that that was his trigger and he had to stay away from him, but he'd say, 'I grew up with him. I can't just ignore him.' So, he would always go when he called. Man, I had so much anger over that guy."

Laurie and Joe never had kids. She goes back and forth now wondering whether this was a good thing or a bad thing in light of Joe's addiction. I ask her to tell me about the hopeful moments when she thought Joe might actually have a chance to beat it.

"It's funny because in his family there's a set of triplets and a set of twins, and I'm a triplet myself," she says. "We wanted kids, but I've had lots of health issues that made it impossible. I used to think, 'Well, if we had kids maybe Joe wouldn't have gotten into the drugs,' but then I think, 'Thank God we didn't have kids so they didn't have to go through all that.' I've got a lot of nieces and nephews, though, so I'm good.

"When Joe got out of rehab in Huntington that first time, he was good. He was back to himself. But he ended up hurting his back at work and then his friend gave him some pills to manage the pain." She sighs, "Eventually, he started taking trips to Florida and telling me it was for work. One time, he wanted to take my car, but I refused because I just couldn't believe his story. I was working afternoon shifts, though, so he came and got the car while I was at work. He ended up calling me from a number I didn't recognize in Florida. I called back and asked for Joe, and the woman who answered said she didn't know any Joe but that she had just let some guy borrow her phone.

Well, I figured out where he was, so when he called back I told him I knew he was down there buying drugs, and that if he didn't have my car back by the time I got off work the next day, I was gonna send the cops looking for him. Well, he came back, but he blew up my car on the way.

"It wasn't long after that when he started the heroin. He got busted for dealing and went to prison for two years. After he got out, he was good again. That was in 2012. He went through STAR [STAR Community Justice Center in Franklin Furnace] before they released him. He had a few good friends who passed away during that time, though, as well as his mom, and I think that really bothered him. Joe went to prison in May of 2010, and she died in September that same year.

"He stayed clean for about three years after that. He had some health problems, but he was able to go back to work. I think that was around the end of May. Then he got MRSA [Methicillin Resistant Staphylococcus Aureus infection] in his knee and ended up in the hospital again on the Fourth of July weekend. They sent him to Columbus for surgery, and then he came back here for six weeks of follow-up. It was hard because his veins were so bad. Home care people had to come in and take care of him. Well, after that he got a bone infection in his wrist from another injury and that took another six weeks in a few different hospitals.

"We got through it, though, and he was good until April of this year. In the spring, we took a trip to see my best friend. We stayed with her for a couple nights and then drove to D.C. to see the cherry blossoms that Saturday. Joe slept in the car the whole way there and back. I was like, 'What's wrong?' He told me he was just tired. He did seem to be better on Sunday, but then he slept the entire drive home the next morning, too, like seven hours.

"When we were just about home, his friend called. I said, 'No. There's no way you're going over there. You've been comatose for two days.' Joe tried to tell me the guy needed help with something—somebody broke into his house or something—but I was like, 'No, you're not doing it.' I just had a feeling something bad was going on. His sister ended up giving him a ride, though. I was so mad I wouldn't let him in the house when they got back. Oh, it was bad. The cops came, but Joe slept in the garage that night. I went and saw a lawyer at that point. I'd gone to see one a couple times before that, but I just never could bring myself to do it. I loved Joe so much."

I nod my head as if to say I understand. "How did Joe's condition affect you?" I ask.

Laurie answers quickly. "Oh—anxiety. Bad anxiety. It was so hard trying to work and pay the bills and keep everything going. I even learned to put up hay to work off one of Joe's debts!" she chuckles. "I got pretty good at it, too. I was able to throw bales around like it was nothing. In fact, I learned to do a lot of things over the last few years that I never thought I would. Painting, fixing things—I'm a workaholic now. I usually sleep for two hours at a time at the most. I'll do things just to keep busy.

"I did drink a lot for a while there, too. Like, a lot, a lot. I remember this one time I got drunk and thought, 'I'm leaving.' I packed my Jeep plumb full and drove all the way to Charleston when I suddenly remembered, 'Oh shit, I'm supposed to work!' Then I thought about my dogs and was like, 'What if Joe doesn't come back? Who's gonna take care of them?'" She laughs at herself. "So, I called work and told them to have someone come in for me. I decided I would sleep it off down there. I just didn't think it through, you know? It was crazy."

As surprising as it may sound given Joe's history, on the evening of October 31, 2018 when he overdosed, drugs were the last thing on Laurie's mind. When the end finally came, it came quickly and unsuspected.

"When I found him, I didn't even think drugs," Laurie says. "It didn't enter my head because he'd been clean since April. We'd had a good day, too. Really, the whole last week or so was good. We visited a few friends that week and talked about all the old stuff we used to do together. Saw all kinds of people whom we hadn't seen in a while. That Wednesday, we went to Spirit Halloween in Ashland—he was Slash and I was his groupie," she grins sheepishly, ducking her head as if to acknowledge how silly it sounds. "I got this purple wig and he had his whole hair thing. He kept saying, 'Do you think I need to curl this? It's a little fuzzy looking.'

"After that, we ate at one of our favorite Mexican restaurants, then came home and watched Guns'-n-Roses videos. It was like four o'clock when I went to bed because I had to work midnight shift that evening. Joe was happy and drinking a tall boy. That was his thing. He'd usually have a tall boy every day. I woke up around nine—which is strange, because like I said, I never sleep more than two hours at a time—and went to shut the back door to the laundry room where we keep the dogs in. That's when I found him lying in the floor between the island and the stove.

"I was like, 'Holy crap!' I thought he had choked on something. I didn't even think about drugs. I went to flip him over to see if there was anything in his mouth and that's when I saw the needle in his hand. He must have fallen straight back, because he banged the back of his head and his knuckles were all busted from falling.

"I yelled, 'No, Joe, no!' and called 911. I had a NARCAN® kit they'd given us like four years ago. It was one of those nasal things, but I couldn't figure out how to use it. I don't know if it had been sitting too long or what, because when I tried to use it, it just busted.

The first responders told me it was probably too late by then, anyway, because Joe was already grey. When I did chest compressions on him, he was gurgling. The fire squad showed up in no time, and they tried everything they could, but it was just too late."

Laurie sighs more deeply now than at any point in our conversation.

"It helps that we had such a good week," she says, smiling through the tears. "Most of the time I'm good because I keep busy. I spend a lot of time at my mom and dad's because they only live ten minutes away. I just … I don't know. I just keep busy. When it came to Joe's addiction, I never could understand it. I'd never done anything like that myself, so I always told him, 'Joe, just stop. It's just a choice.' But he'd say, 'You don't understand; it's not that easy.' And I didn't understand. He tried to get me to go to counseling to talk to people, but I figured if it wasn't helping him, why should I go? I've read lots of stuff, though. I've gotten on Google and looked at articles. Plus the things he sent me, like when he was in prison and would write me letters telling me everything he felt. But … I never could understand it."

As I listen to Laurie share the final chapter of Joe's story, I remind myself that what she's telling me only happened a few months prior to our conversation. In fact, I recall seeing the news of Joe's passing—though I didn't know him or Laurie at the time—on Facebook the day after he died. I think back to where I was the night when they were spending their final moments together, and I try to imagine how I'd feel being in Laurie's shoes with the person I love more than anything else in the whole world lying dead on the ground in front of me. It hurts. I don't want to end their story with the sadness of Joe's passing' however, so I ask for one final memory.

"When you think of Joe now," I say, "what comes to your mind?"

Laurie responds immediately: "His smile. Joe had such a beautiful smile." She takes a deep breath, then wipes the corner of her eye with one hand. As she does, I think of all the people I know who have done things I couldn't understand when they were caught up in the throes of addiction. Feeling what I assume to be the same strange mixture of love and regret, I smile at her.

"Joe was such a kind-hearted person," she says. "Everyone loved him. Even through the drugs and everything, everybody loved him."

"I'M JUST A GIRL."

O f all the people I interviewed for this book, Christine was the most eager to share her story with me. She reached out to me first through Facebook, and she kept reaching out until we were able to nail down a time to get together. Her enthusiasm for helping people who struggle with addiction is palpable.

It was bitterly cold the morning we met in the lobby of the Ironton Holiday Inn in early 2019. Christine was light-hearted but all business. We found a quiet place in the conference room where we could talk uninterrupted, and she began by telling me about the last time she overdosed—November 2017.

⊖ ⊖ ⊖

"T oward the end of my addiction I was using heroin," Christine says. "I actually ended up in the hospital with a spinal infection because of it. I still wasn't ready to quit, though. I was dealing dope out of the hospital room! I checked myself out to keep from going to jail. I went home, and later that night was when my daughter and son-in-law pulled me out of a tub of water where I had overdosed and fell over. I woke up to my son crying and screaming, 'Mom, please wake up!' I had been gone for six minutes.

"Stephen and I are close and he's always been very protective of me. I think a lot of it has to do with everything he witnessed growing up—the abuse and dysfunction." She pauses. "He kept his distance there at the end because he had a new baby and he didn't want him to be exposed, so I don't have a great relationship with my only grandson because of it. But it's time to rebuild, and now that's finally possible.

"I was in Columbus when I overdosed. After waking up in the hospital, I had a nurse who was really infuriated with me. I was freezing and they kept putting warm blankets on me—from all the NARCAN®. But he got mad because I was asking for more blankets. He literally yanked that bed out and started wheeling me down the hallway and said, 'You're going to the morgue. You think you're cold now, but this is where you're headed.' Then he wheeled me back. That was an eye-opener."

I ask whether Christine thinks the nurse was just reacting out of anger or whether he was genuinely trying to help her see the outcome of her choices. She thinks it was the latter. Either way, it didn't make much of an immediate difference.

"I went home and did another shot," she says flatly. "That's exactly what I did. My son took me home, and I went in and did another shot. The next morning, I wanted to check myself into detox, so I started calling places for treatment. Everyone kept telling me to call back or that they would put me on a waiting list, though. I wasn't getting anywhere.[1] Finally, I found a bed at Talbot Hall. They gave me a resource list, and on the back page I found information for a place called Land of Goshen in Ironton. I called them and they took me right away. That's how I ended up here. Best decision of my life."

---

1   I'd be remiss here if I didn't point out the disparity between treatment and incarceration as a response to addiction. If Christine had been arrested while she was in the hospital, they would have found a bed for her in jail even if they had to double her up with someone else. Finding a bed for treatment took a little more work. Ohio still has a long way to go to address this shortfall.

Christine had been abusing drugs in one form or another for thirty-five years before she arrived at treatment in 2017. I ask about the impact this had not only on her but on her family.

"I think what kept me using all those years was the guilt and the shame over what I was doing to my family," she says. "I felt like I would be better off dead. Like I should do everybody a favor and just be gone. That's where addiction takes you. You deal with so much guilt and shame that it makes you feel unworthy of anything, even of living. I pretty much isolated everyone through the years. I ran them all off. I robbed everyone. I broke their trust. There was no one who wanted anything to do with me. That includes friends, family— people I'd known for twenty, thirty years. They loved me and told me they loved me, that they knew I was a better person than I was acting, but they still didn't want nothing to do with me. I don't blame them. I wouldn't have, either.

"Now, however, it's amazing. My son comes here to see me. They come down once a month or every other month. My entire family does. This past Christmas was the first one I spent with my entire family. Fifty years old, first Christmas ever with my kids and I was sober. I could finally sit with my brothers and sisters and my mom, and they weren't ashamed of me. I was no longer that toxic person in their life."

"How does that feel?" I ask.

Christine smiles wide. "It's pretty amazing," she says. "Yeah. I thought the bridges were burned completely. My addiction kept telling me that it was too late, that I'd done too much. But it's never too late. After thirty-five years of addiction, even, it's never too late.

"I was married at sixteen. That's when I was introduced to IV drugs. I married into a crime family, which I didn't know before. But I found out very quickly. By the age of twenty-one, I had lost my first child and was introduced to prostitution. I was raped three times." Her voice quivers. "I watched my mother-in-law overdose. That was after a night of doing dope together. We thought she was sleeping, but she passed away. When we went to her room to wake her up, she had been laying there dead for five hours. The whole time we were sitting there getting high.

"My husband spiraled out of control after that and ended up in prison for burglary. We separated, and I got into another toxic relationship with an abusive man. I thought that was normal, so I continued abusing drugs and it kept cycling over and over. I ended up with five kids before I finally left him. We buried him a few years ago. Heroin-induced heart attack. One year later, I buried my niece, who died in Ross County jail due to complications from heroin withdrawal.[2]

"Before I ever started using drugs, though, my life was full of dysfunction. I'm the oldest of ten in my family. We always had cousins and aunts and uncles living with us. Lots of family, lots of partying. My mom had me when she was fifteen. I know she did the best she could being that age, but there was a lot of dysfunction and chaos.

"Do you have any positive memories?" I ask.

"I don't remember having any aspirations for my life," Christian says. "I was given a lot of adult responsibilities before I was even grown up. I just remember wanting to go out and be with my friends and play and stuff like that. I never really made it to school. If I did, it was in one door and out the other. I do remember getting three trophies one year from basketball. Other than that, my childhood was

---

2   Statistically, the likelihood that a person will overdose or die from other drug-related health complications goes up in jail. Those who are unable to obtain drugs in jail are also at a higher risk for overdose immediately after release due to their decreased tolerance level. All the more reason to reform the criminal justice system.

pretty crappy. My parents never showed up to school events or games. There was always fighting at home. All the drinking and partying and using was my normal. It was the cool thing to do. If I would have had a role model, or more mentorship in my life—that would have made a big difference. Someone to look up to. That, and getting rewarded for doing good. I think that's what a lot of kids are missing."

When Christine walked through the doors at Land of Goshen for the first time, she was mentally and emotional exhausted.

"I just felt tired," she says. "I had no emotions. I was kind of numb. I think I was just ready to take a break from using. I didn't know at that point if I was ready to quit entirely. I was just going to take a break, get my health back, and then maybe go back to using. I didn't know. Either way, I thought my life was over. I figured that dying as a junkie was all I had to look forward to. I had accepted that. But slowly, the people at Goshen worked with me and showed me that I was worth so much more than that. They stood beside me. They saw so much more in me than I had ever been told about myself. I'd always been told that I was a failure who would never amount to anything. I never felt like God hated me, but I also didn't think He really liked me, either. But they stood with me and they loved me until I could love myself."

Christine's voice cracks. Her eyes fill with tears.

"It was so amazing," she says. "Now, all I want to do is give other addicts what they gave me. Because I know what it's like. You can't just quit using drugs and go on. You have to get rid of the behaviors and the attitudes and that old mindset. You have to rewire yourself. And it's possible! If I can do it after thirty-five years, anybody can do it. I'm not special. Details of each person's story may be different, you know—some may be more graphic than others, for instance—but what is it that's the same in every story? The guilt, the shame, and the feeling of unworthiness. We all share that same pain.

"My recovery was slow-going at first," she says. "It took a few months. I had to go back to the hospital and battle the spinal infection. I was only at Goshen ten days before I got put back in the hospital. They shipped me to Cincinnati, Ashland, West Virginia. It was 6-8 weeks of treatment.

"After all that, though, one day I was sitting in a group with Mark at Land of Goshen. He looked me in the eye and said, 'You're not a failure. You are worthy. You are loved. And you can do anything you want to do.' When he said that, something clicked. It's always stuck with me. It made me feel like somebody." Her voice breaks again. "That made a big difference. Just to look a kid in the eye—because at fifty years old, that's what I felt like—and say, 'You're not a failure. You're worth so much more than people have told you.' To hear that for the first time ever at fifty years old … that was pretty amazing."

"What role does shame play in all of this?" I ask.

"Shame breaks a person down to make them feel like they're nothing," Christine says. "Like they're not worthy to even be alive. If you have someone who is struggling with addiction, just let them know that no matter what, they are still loved. I had a lot of family and friends tell me that they wished I was dead. They would say, 'Are you ever gonna OD the right way? You can't even commit suicide right!' But just knowing you are loved is so important. If you have someone in addiction, let them know that you see them for who they really are, not the person who is doing those things. A lot of this comes down to the issue of identity. People will act according to who they believe themselves to be."

Christine's long-term goal is to open a safe house where people can stay for a few weeks while they are waiting to get into treatment. This desire coincides with the general need for transitional living that I've heard many other people in recovery talk about.

"I feel like my purpose is to be out in the midst of addiction and reaching those addicts who are ready now," Christine says. "I don't want to be sitting in an office in a clinic. There are just too many people who are never gonna walk in and ask for help. So, I feel that I need to go meet them where they're at and give them hope. But when I'm talking to somebody, and they tell me they are ready, I don't have anywhere to put them. Transitional living is a big obstacle for people who are ready to get help. That's my goal.

"There's a lot of details to work out—getting grants and stuff and figuring out how to handle people in different situations. But that's ok. I hustled to get dope, so now I can hustle to do legal stuff." She laughs. "I'm doing that kind of thing already when I help organize our 'Come to the Table' community event. I'm out hustling to get donations and gift cards and catering and all this stuff. It's sad, but I've found more people in the bars willing to help than I have in the churches."

As unfortunate as this is to hear, I can't dispute Christine's findings about the faith community. There are exceptions, of course. For instance, Christine has worked a lot with the folks at Real Life Ministries in Ironton, Ohio. Christ Episcopal Church is heavily involved in recovery work throughout Lawrence County, and Land of Goshen is a faith-based organization.

"People don't realize how hard it is to maintain a drug addiction," Christine continues. "I was out hustling every day to get the money and the drugs I needed. But the shame I felt over stuff I had to do was just overwhelming. Most people who steal from others to maintain their addiction aren't criminals. In other words, they wouldn't be doing these things if they weren't being driven by their addiction.

That's why people are so amazed when they meet me today and hear about my past. A year and a half ago, I was a junkie. I was taking a needle and shooting up a gram of heroin a day. Now, people look at me when they hear that and go, 'Huh?' They just can't see it. That's how much addiction changes you. My friends and family who knew me then, though—they know. For instance, I had my daughter look at me ..."

Christine begins to break down again. Her voice quivers and she has to force the words out. "I saw her looking at me, and it was finally, 'Mom, I'm *proud* of you.' I didn't have to say anything. She saw the change in me. She saw the difference. Today, my family sees someone they can be proud of for the first time ever, and I just want other moms to have the same experience. My kids are grown now, but others ... we've got to spare the kids. Because if we don't deal with our monsters, we're just gonna pass them down to our kids. *We've got stop feeding our demons to our children.*

"My two youngest kids got put on medicine for separation anxiety and night terrors. All they wanted was their mom. I truly believe they developed mental illnesses because of my choices. So, if I can help one mother spare her kids from that ... Am I rebuilding now? Yes, absolutely. Is it amazing? Yes, absolutely. But there are bonds I broke in the past that can never be fully repaired. Parents need to know how to be a role model in their children's lives. That means so much to them as they develop their identity. They need to know that they can do anything they want, and that they are loved and they are important."

As our conversation winds down, Christine turns the interview around and asks me what I think it will take to break down the stigma and shame that keeps addicted people from getting help. How do we make society see that people with substance use disorder need compassionate care and not punishment? How do we get folks who have never experienced drug addiction, or the kind of trauma that often leads to it, to care about people like herself?

"I'm just a girl," Christine pleads. "I'm not an 'addict.' I'm not some piece of trash. I didn't *choose* to go through the things I went through. Who would?"

Of course, I hardly know what to say. But something inside me—the same drive that led me to write *The Face of Addiction*—believes that it all comes down to the stories we tell ourselves about addiction and addicted people. The cultural narrative I grew up with led me to believe that people who use drugs were essentially moral degenerates, the kind who lived in dark alleyways and crack houses and would never amount to anything in life other than being a public nuisance. The only solution society gave me to the problem of drug addiction as a child in the 1980's was to "just say no." I've come to see that it is far more complex than that.

So, yes, we can and should advocate for increased funding for treatment, the passage of humane criminal justice reform, legal prosecution of pharmaceutical companies, and the implementation of evidence-based treatment. But the root of the issue is deeper. The source of addiction lies in the general fragmentation of society and its failure to provide for healthy human development. Every civilization is built on certain cultural narratives that inform how we understand and relate to one another, and frankly, our current story surrounding addiction is wholly inadequate to meet the needs of people engulfed in this crisis. Until that story shifts in such a way to change how we see the world, people will continue to fall through the cracks and die. That is why I wrote this book. It is why I support people like Christine. I may be able to write complete sentences and put a manuscript together, but she has the kind of lived experience that people desperately need to hear.

"Anyone can reach me on Facebook," she says, "or they can call me. I make my phone number public on there. I make it available to anyone at any time. I know my story reaches a lot of people, so my phone is always on and I always answer it for that reason. It takes a lot of courage to make that call for help, so someone has to answer when they do."

"GET BUSY WITH YOUR LIFE AND STOP THINKING ABOUT YOUR ADDICTION."

Jan is one of those people who tells it like it is and doesn't care what you think about it. She knows what works for her and what doesn't, and at the end of the day that's good enough for her. Any new information you give her is going to be processed through the filter of her own hard-fought experience. If it passes the test, then great. If it doesn't compute, well, she'll just table it and move on.

It was dreary the day I visited Jan at her home. She met me on the front porch and invited me inside, showing me through the living room to the kitchen table. We sat down together and stumbled through a few moments of small talk. Finally, I pulled out my notebook and asked how her battle with addiction first began. She tapped her cigarette over the ash tray that was sitting between us and took my cue.

⊖ ⊖ ⊖

"We didn't have the word 'addiction' back then," Jan begins. "I started drinking when I was thirteen, but I was in a car wreck when I was eighteen. That was in May of 1981. They gave me morphine in the hospital and sent me home with three bottles. I remember getting really sick after it ran out. The doctor told my mother I was just drinking too much of it, but you don't recognize what's really going on.

"Later on in my life, around 1997-98, when I moved back home from Savannah, GA with my ex-husband, he was taking pills following an accident where he fell off a fifteen-foot scaffold. I had some back issues and was hurting from all the unpacking, so he told me I could take one of his pills if I needed to. I thought, 'Well, I'll just break it in half.' I took that first half and was like, 'Oh, wow.' The next day I was still hurting, so I took the other half. I wondered, 'If half a pill does this for me, what's a whole pill gonna do?' Then one becomes two, and so on. That's where it began.

"My husband was a patient of Dr. Proctor, a guy who would hand out prescriptions easily with no questions asked. The money he made from his philosophy brought in more doctors just like him. My ex was selling and trading his pills like lots of other people at the time. Later on, he told me about the money you could make and that I needed to get my own doctor." She hesitates. "I'm trying to remember who my first doctor was, but I couldn't even tell you. There were so many. I never saw Proctor because he was already in trouble around that time.

"Anyway, I'd been diagnosed with Fibromyalgia in Savannah, which just means they don't know why you hurt, but they're gonna put a label on you. It helped me get what I needed once I started seeing those doctors. Going to the pill mill doctors was awkward, though, because I didn't know how to play the game. I had no clue what I was doing. I had to be coached on what to do and say at first, like how to respond when they ask you how much pain you feel or how far you can push their hand."

Jan reaches her hand out in my direction as if to mimic the motion she is describing.

"That's how you got in with the doctors," she continues, "by learning how to pretend. I was legitimately hurting, you know, but not like I saw the others hurting. It was just awkward. But I learned quickly.

"I began to spiral out of control within a matter of months. At one point, it would take eight narcos just to get me out of bed." She chuckles, but not in a way that indicates genuine amusement. "Yeah, that's a lot. But I couldn't function without that many. Then when you see dollar signs, it's easy to get into it even more. I saw how much profit I could make off those pills. It's a sick game you have to play, though, because you also want to keep them for yourself. You're gonna sell this many, but then you've lost that many and you're gonna need them again. The chase is the worst part."

"The chase?" I ask.

"Oh, it was horrible. I mean, it was fun in one sense—you know, the cat-and-mouse game. I think you get more addicted to the game than you do to the pill. The chase is addictive in itself."

Jan takes a long drag from her cigarette.

"But I should go back," she says. "The reason I say that I'm every cliché is because I'm from a divorced family, my mother decided to move us into a trailer court, and I got pregnant at fifteen. At eighteen, I had my wreck. The guy who was with me suffered serious damage to his frontal lobe. He would get angry because he wasn't the same anymore after the wreck, so he would take it out on me. The car wreck messed with my head, too. We hit a tree going about a hundred miles per hour. All the trauma I experienced that night—it really plays in your head for the rest of your life. To this day I have issues resulting from that night. I can take you to the place where it happened. I think part of my soul died there that night. I became numb in life, so drugs came easy for me.

"Yeah," she chuckles again in that "funny, not funny" sort of way, "I've been married three times, and all of them had their hand in one deal or another. Drugs have always been a part of my life. You know, it's like when you're eighteen you're supposed to see a path in life. Most people choose a career. I wanted to go in that direction, but, for some reason, I went a different way whether I wanted to or not. I was stuck in the tornado of the whole thing. I wanted to go to Columbus and work at Nationwide, the tallest and most beautiful building in the city. I could type and take shorthand dictation at 120 words per minute. After the car wreck, though, I couldn't do that anymore. I still wanted to get there, but I just kept going on this other path to the point that I was blinded. It was just more fun—the drinking and drugs and running around. It was more fun than going to college and starting a career. The sad thing is, there was a little boy who was being affected by it all ... mine.

"I did have some support. My mother really stepped up and took care of my son. I always kept my family away from my habits, though. I didn't want them to see me high or see me struggling, so I pushed my son away to keep him safe. And now because of that, we don't have a close relationship. In fact, he kind of resents me. The way I tried to protect him was by not letting anyone know about him, or anyone in my family for that matter. When I was in the 'drug world,' I didn't talk about my family. That was off limits. I told everybody, 'My son's a prick and my mother's a bitch. Don't even talk about them.' I wanted them to think there was a wall there that they couldn't cross, even if they ran into my family out in public."

Jan shifts uncomfortably in her seat, as if she's struggling to find the right words to describe the situation.

"I don't know how to explain it," she says. "He still lived with me during those years, but I just kept it away from him. There was a gap between me and him, though. Now, he resents what I did and he resents the rumors he heard about me. I'm still not a good mom, although I want to be. I'm *awake* now. But it might be too late. We don't hang out or talk very often anymore. I've apologized to him so many times, but he doesn't want to talk about it. I'd love for him to hit me with his best shot—just tell me what he's pissed off about and what he doesn't like about me, you know? But he won't do it."

Jan finally stopped abusing pills in April 2010. The way she tells the story, it was a mixture of divine intervention and practical necessity that led her to quit.

"I was broke," she says. "When God sits you down, God sits you down. My life literally fell apart. I'd always been a functioning addict, so I was able to work to get my money, but it still fell apart. Three things happened: First, I pawned all my gold jewelry to get some cash, then I found out I lost all of it. Second, I totaled my car along with another lady's car. Third, I lost my job. I sat on my swing that day like any other day with so many thoughts in my head. I was lucky enough to score that morning but I had no clue how I was going to score any more. I thought to myself, 'Your game is up. You're done. This is it.' I had no money, no credit, and people weren't gonna pay me what they owed me. So I decided to stop. I walked inside and made up a bed on my couch. I got a trash can, paper towels, tissues, pop, remote control … I just got myself prepared to detox. I locked the door, shut the curtains, and said, 'Here we go.'"

Jan stops to draw on her cigarette before continuing.

"Now, I do not advise anyone to do it that way, ok?" She laughs. "It was the best way for me to do it to get over my addiction, but it ain't smart to do that by yourself. Luckily, there was a woman who lived up

above me who saw how sick I was and knew what I was doing down-
stairs. I would wake up, and she'd be sitting in the chair watching over
me. She would bring me meals from her own dinner in case I felt like
eating, but I hardly did. I was 74 pounds and throwing up water constantly. I was dying. I just knew it was time. I laid there and literally
looked into the pit of hell. I literally saw hell and met my demons. It
wasn't fun. As far as the illness goes, it took about two weeks. After
that, it would be ninety degrees and I'd be outside wrapped up in a
blanket wearing flannel pajamas because I was freezing to death."

It dawns on me while Jan is talking that all of this misery came
about just from taking pills. Jan doesn't remember ever shooting heroin or even snorting it. The closest she came was licking the residue
off the spoons that her friends were using to inject.

Jan continues, "So after that, of course, welfare took care of me.
Someone or something had to. I had two years of clean time. Then
I met another guy online"—she stretches her neck and looks toward
the man sitting in the living room next to us—"who I started talking
to. The first time I saw him, I knew he was taking pills, but I didn't
know the extent of it. When he came to visit me, though, I looked
at him, and I saw *death*. He had the ash-grey look. He was trying to
tough it out that day and not use pills for my sake, but he was sick
because of it. A couple months later I visited him in Nashville where
he lived, and I was so tempted to start back up. You couldn't get pills
anymore in Ohio, but there were over 300 pain clinics in Nashville
at that time. It would have been so easy, but I didn't do it. Eventually,
Kevin stopped using pills, too. We've been together ever since."

Jan keeps mostly to herself nowadays. She maintains no formal
connection to the recovery community because she wants to keep
drugs as far away from her mind as possible. She doesn't attend
Narcotics Anonymous (NA) meetings because she believes that the

message of powerlessness enshrined in the first of the twelve steps is ultimately self-defeating.

"I don't give a shit what they say," she explains. "During your addiction, you are *not* powerless over it. You have the power, you're just ignoring it. I think more than anything else, that message gives people permission to relapse. They think, 'Oh, I'm just sick. I'm powerless.' Well, no, you're not. You *can* get it together."

This perspective intrigues me. I think of SMART Recovery and other cognitive-based forms of addiction treatment that operate with a similar philosophy. Jan's conviction highlights the fact that there are multiple valid paths to recovery. What works for some people does not necessarily work for others.

"I do think NA helps some people," she continues. "But it's not for me. And I don't know anyone who goes to meetings because I don't know anyone. I have one friend who I talk to who has struggled with addiction for a long time. But I literally don't want to leave this house. I don't want to go anywhere beyond my yard. I don't want to run into anybody. I don't want to deal with it. I've lost way too many people. This epidemic has taken a lot of lives, and, unfortunately, I helped start it. I made a lot of mistakes. I hurt a lot of people. Mainly my son and myself."

Fair enough, I think, then look down at my notebook for a final question. Something tells me Jan has already given more mental energy to this subject than she would care to, and I don't want to impose on her time.

I ask, "If you could go back in time and tell your younger self one thing to spare you all those years of suffering, what would it be?"

Jan snorts. "It wouldn't make a difference," she says. "Finding peace of mind in the present is what matters now. Of course, I do regret the part I played in the opiate epidemic as a dealer, and I do believe that society could be addressing it better now, like with more beds and better access to treatment. But I want no part in that effort myself."

This is exactly what I mean by saying that Jan is the kind of person who tells it like it is and doesn't care what you think. She's content to stick with her own personal philosophy, and whether I agree with it or not, I admire this trait. Jan has been on disability since 2010, so the only work she does these days is gardening in her front yard. Being out in the sunshine with her grandkids is what brings her the most joy in life. Out there under the sun, the medical model of addiction as a chronic brain disease is, by all accounts, far from her mind. If I had to sum up her entire message to people with substance use disorder in a single line, I couldn't say it any better than she did at the end of our conversation.

Leaning forward in her chair, Jan looks me right in the eye and says, "Get busy with life and stop thinking about your addiction." Then she pauses, perhaps for dramatic effect, and repeats herself. "Get busy, and let it go."

"ALL I WANT FOR CHRISTMAS IS MY DADDY."

John is what they call a straight shooter. He is one of the most unassuming guys I've ever met. If he has something to say, he'll say it. If not, he won't pretend or put on a show. Pretense just doesn't seem to be part of his game anymore. Oh, I'm sure he faked it quite a bit back in the day to support his addiction, but I didn't know him then. I've only heard from other people how astounding his transformation has been. According to one guy, whose story features prominently at the end of this book, John is the "exception." He is living proof that there is, as he often likes to say, "hope after dope."

⊖ ⊖ ⊖

"I grew up in McDermott, which is a small town," John begins. "When I was younger, it was probably 1,500 people, if that. I had a good family. Mom stayed at home till I was fifteen or sixteen. Dad worked his fingers to the bone to support fourteen kids. Neither one of them were addicts. They did what they had to do make sure we had food on the table. Dad only had a seventh grade education, so he was a garbage man, repair man, gardener, whatever he could do. He was the kind of guy who took care of anybody who needed it. If people couldn't afford food, he would give it to them right out of his garden.

"I was just a normal kid. I played sports—football, baseball, basketball, and track. Perfect attendance at school. When people approached me about doing drugs, I'd say, 'Get that away from me. I'm gonna play in the NBA one day!'" He smiles. "That was my goal. It's what I wanted to do."

"But then during my sophomore year, I was out one day and ran into a group of friends who were all standing in a circle. I remember this like it was yesterday because it changed my whole life. I walked up to see what they were talking about because they were all laughing and having a good time. Well, they were passing around weed. The crazy part is, nobody tried to push it on me. As they were passing it around, one of the guys even grabbed it before it came to me and said, 'He don't smoke.' I guess my pride stepped in, because I said, 'Give me that.' I tried it that day.

"Everyone in my neighborhood was smoking weed by this time. Or doing acid, or something. It was around 1993 or 1994 and that's how it started for me. I still stuck with basketball as much as I could, but nobody else wanted to play ball anymore. So, it started progressing. I ended up going to Vo-Tech, and during my junior year I was intro-duced to pills. I only made it till Christmas break that year 'cause I got kicked out for talking back to a teacher. It was something simple, but it changed my life. I got a letter in the mail saying I wasn't allowed back for two years. When I tried to return to Northwest, they told me I'd have to repeat freshman math. My pride stepped in again, and I refused to take the class over. I dropped out instead.

"Then, on the night of the Super Bowl that year I was introduced to cocaine. I was out partying when my Dad showed up and said, 'You start work tomorrow morning in Columbus at 7 AM.' My brother-in-law had a construction company, and he offered me a job for $9 an hour. I was like, 'Dad, I ain't going nowhere.'" John chuckles. "My dad was a big guy, so you didn't tell him 'no' too much. I left the party and got up the next morning for work.

"So I went up there, just turned eighteen, and I'm making $9 an hour starting out. I ain't got no family at this time, no kids, no girl-friend, so I started putting money in the bank. I was working 70-80 hours a week 'cause I didn't have nothing else to do. The only thing I did was drive back down to McDermott every weekend to get my bag of weed. And that's where my drug of choice came into play. I stared using nerve pills—Xanax, Valium. They got ahold of me more than any other drug. I just felt more myself, like I was *me*. I was more comfortable." He pauses, evidently searching for words. "I don't know, they just took ahold of me. I felt like I could be myself without wor-rying what other people think. Being an addict, you know, it comes with a label. People start to think, 'What good are you?' The nerve pills helped me face that stigma because then I just didn't care.

"As the weeks go by, I'm coming home every weekend and getting introduced to new drugs. But then I had some trouble with one of the guys I was working with in Columbus. One day he pushed me too far, and I was ready to kill him, so instead of getting into trouble, I just left and went back home. Worst decision I ever made. I was making good money, but it started to dissipate fast. That's when I was introduced to another drug they called 'bathtub crank.' It was crystal meth, pretty much.

"Me and some friends really got into that drug. I called it my 'seven-day theory' because I was on it for seven straight days." John shakes his head and appears to be disgusted at this memory. "I didn't eat, sleep … I didn't do nothing but try to figure out how to stay high. We were robbing things—anything that wasn't bolted down, really. I mean, I was more of a manipulator. I would talk other people into doing it. But for seven days, that's what we did. Then I started hallucinating. I was seeing ambulances and stuff like that. My heart started racing. But the night before I finally did get some sleep, I took some guys to rob a house. I remember one of the guys saying he got caught on camera and we had to get rid of everything because the Law was gonna show up. Sure enough, at 7:00 the next morning, the Law was beating on the door. They were asking whose car was sitting outside, which was mine, so I took off. I made it home that day, but I got arrested a couple days later.

"I still remember that first ten days in jail thinking, 'This ain't for me.' I don't know how many people realize it, but the old Scioto County jail was full of drugs. They were carrying people out on gurneys. And there I was, nineteen years old, seeing that for the first time. It was pretty crazy. Of course, when I came out, I had the best of intentions. I said I wasn't gonna get high. But I only made it till that night. By then, someone had done found out I was out of jail and was asking me to get high. So I did, but I tried to keep it to just weed. Next to Xanax—that was my go-to. But I learned that as someone who has an addictive personality, I couldn't just smoke weed and get away with it.

"So, in a couple weeks I was back to doing what I was doing. I didn't mess with crystal meth anymore, though. It really did something to me physically, to my heart. I think I had a stroke, honestly. My anxiety got real bad after that. I couldn't breathe. I'd have to walk outside. It really messed me up mentally. But with that increased anxiety now, it made me want to do more nerve pills so I could feel better. So I went back into doing Xanax and got real bad on them. I was eating ten bars every morning before my feet even hit the floor. By then the pill doctors had starting coming in. Most people don't realize this, but the pill mills were around years before they caught public attention."[3]

"So, that went on for a while until I caught a charge for theft of the elderly and forgery at twenty-two. I didn't do what they said I did, but I wasn't gonna snitch on the other guys either. I had two kids by that time. My oldest boy was just born and all I could think about was, 'I need to get home to my kids.' Of course I've got an addiction problem, but I'm not seeing that. I'm still young and I've got the wool pulled over my eyes. I'm blinded by it, but I'm still trying to get home to my kids."

"In the first hearing, I was facing five years in prison. By the end, they agreed to give me twelve months total with six months already served in the county jail. When they made that offer, I said, 'Let's do it. I didn't write those bad checks, but if this will get me home to my kids in less than a year, let's do it.' I signed the papers and they sent me to prison boot camp. I figured it was an opportunity to try to get my life right. If it was something educational, I felt like it could be a turning point. I told my family, and they were about as excited as you can be when someone you love is going to jail.

"I finished my time and went to a halfway house afterwards. Whenever I came home, I had a clear mind. I was healthy. I quit smoking. I was ready to take life on. So, I get a place in Oak Hill for my kids and their mother and start working. She's taking care of the kids and then ends up pregnant again.

"Now, I'm on parole, so I gotta check in three times a week. That doesn't leave much room for error, but it does hold me accountable.

---

3   I recall going to a community march in 2010 that was meant to draw attention to Portsmouth's pill mill problem. That was when they began getting public attention. But John had been going to local doctors as far back as 1998.

About ten months in, though, I get hurt at work. I go to the doctor, and they prescribe me Tylenol 3s. My addiction, which I thought was over, came knocking at the door again. I started going out looking for more of these pills, but I couldn't find them. So one day my brother, who was also an addict and had gone to a pain clinic, gave me some Percocet.

"I took them," he says, snapping his finger, "and automatically, that addiction kicked in. I felt like I was Superman, like I was just a kid again. Of course, I'm only twenty-three at the time, but I felt *good*. Things started spiraling out of control again that night. One leads to three, three leads to ten, and before you know it, I'm back on my nerve pills."

Or, as I've heard so many people say in these interviews, *it progressed*.

In November 2006, John's dad died.

"Dad was my best friend, my superhero," John says. "The day before he died, I had a bottle of pills in my pocket that fell out while I was at my parent's house. My mom found it and gave it to my dad. We argued about it, and I lied to him and said that the pills belonged to someone else. I manipulated him into giving me the pills back, and that's the last conversation we ever had.

"I remember waking up the next morning to put my kids on the bus. Our neighbor came out and asked where a certain address was. I said, 'That's us, why?' and he said, 'It just came over the scanner that someone died.' Before the words were even out of his mouth, I was in a dead sprint back to the house, and sure enough, when I get there, my dad had passed away.

"All that mattered after that was doing that bottle of pills. Not only them, but anything else I could get my hands on. I didn't think about my kids or my mom or my brothers and sisters. I didn't think about what they were going through. And I believe wholeheartedly that I overdosed that night. I remember falling on my knees and seeing a premonition of my death. I could see daylight up through the ground and my kids playing in the yard above me.

"It was enough to scare me straight, for a little while at least. I stayed clean that time for twenty-one days. Eventually, though, I started sneaking drinks and Xanax again. It was pride, I guess. People kept telling me how good I looked, and for some reason I didn't like that. It's like they saw me as a recovering addict and nothing else. I wanted them to see me as more than that … as a person. So when they said things like, 'Did you learn your lesson?' I just resented it and decided to start using again."

Life went on that way for a while. John met a girl who tried to help him with his addiction, but their relationship was short-lived. Then he met his now ex-wife. The first night they went out, John got so high (to help relieve his anxiety) that he poured his drink on her. She forgave him, and eventually they married. In 2009, she was arrested for an outstanding warrant on a speeding ticket. John went to visit her, and on his way home, he accidentally struck a group of teenagers who were walking on Dogwood Ridge in Wheelersburg. When the dust settled from that incident, John was left facing four years in prison on charges that included three level 5 felonies and one level 3 felony. The judge granted a stay of execution so he could go home for thirty days prior to sentencing.

"There I was with my kids in front of Miller Manor Apartments," John says, "and they're crying because I'm telling them I have to leave them. I'm having to tell them, 'Daddy messed up, and now I have to take ownership of it.' Knowing I was going to jail gave me even more reason to party, though. The day of my trial, I got a handful of Oxy's. My mom showed up and asked if I needed a ride to court. I looked at the pills in my hand and decided to get high before I went in. My addiction told me, 'You can miss the hearing. As long as you turn yourself in, you'll be alright.' Of course, that was far from the truth. It might work for some people, but it didn't work for me. I stayed away for about a month, but one day I was at Wayne Hills when the officer pulled up. I didn't try to run. I just walked up to the SUV and got in. They gave me the full eight years, mandatory. When I got to prison, though, it was still 'poor, pitiful me.'"

The way John talks about his addiction as if it's something outside of himself reminds me of the old cultural image of the devil on one's shoulder, whispering in his ear with the voice of temptation. In this case, that voice led John to the Ross County Correctional Facility. His first five months there was business as usual. He stayed clean for a little while but soon got into trouble for running with the wrong crowd. He bought a television from another inmate on credit, but the money his wife was supposed to send him to pay it off never showed up. As a result, he was forced to make "jailhouse whiskey" to cover his debt. That move landed him in the hole. You wouldn't guess it from the sound of things, but this is precisely where John's story finally changes for the better.

"While I'm in the hole, I get a letter from my daughter," he says. "It was a letter to Santa Claus saying, '*All I want for Christmas is my daddy.*' That changed my life. Right there in that cell is where I began to re-evaluate who I was as a person. Everything in my life—and I'm sugarcoating a lot of it for this story, you have to understand—everything led to this moment in that 8-by-8 cell. Here I am, thinking 'poor, pitiful me' when I had four beautiful children who now had to fend for themselves and look to somebody else for comfort and guidance. That thought didn't sit well with me because my kids were my life. Always have been, always will be.

"From that day on, I gave my life to God. When I came out of the hole, I got baptized. I got into GED classes. I always thought I was the dumbest person in the world, but I buckled down. I had a new drive, a new outlook on life. I wanted that GED more than anything so I could take it home and show my kids. I passed the test on my first try.

"Then, Ross County became a level-three facility, so I ended up at the Chillicothe Correctional unit where there were more opportunities. I went to sign up for college courses, thinking I wouldn't be accepted, but they put me on as the last person on the list. So not only was I taking four college courses, but I also became a mentor in their drug program. This hunger, this drive inside of me took over. Everything they ever told me I wasn't going to do—because I was just an addict, or just this poor guy from McDermott—I decided to do it. Not for them, but for me, my children, and my family.

"I took part in a faith-based program called Horizon. It was ninety-nine guys staying together in one building. You had to do classes together and learn about different religions. My patience really grew a lot during that time. People started to confide in me a lot about what they wanted to achieve, which is how I got started as a mentor. I had a background in construction and home renovations, so that's the approach I took to my personal growth—I was rebuilding. I felt so broken on the inside, but I realized it was up to me to become the man I was supposed to be, the man my dad taught me to be. I got forty-seven total certificates in prison for anything I could learn. Real estate, public speaking—anything they offered. Not just because I wanted to learn myself, but because I wanted to teach my children. I wanted to come home educated so I could help my kids become educated, so they would never choose the life I had chosen to live.

"Toward the end of my prison term, I did self-evaluation probably every other day to make sure I was ready to come home to my kids. That was my drive. Everybody kept telling me I wasn't gonna believe how the world had changed since I was in prison, like how technology had changed in the six years since I was incarcerated. So before I get out, I'm trying to think of things I can do career-wise that's also gonna keep me on the right track of doing what I need to do for my kids. That's how RAW Addiction came about. I figured, 'What better way for the world to hear my story than through social media?' Not only my message, but the message of other people like me, or people like you who are trying to help the community. I'm gonna set a stage for people all over the world to hear these things.

"So, I asked guys who I was mentoring in the prison to tell me about Facebook. They tell me you can be connected with people from all over the world. My wheels start turning. But I also know I gotta get my life straight first. So, the first year I came home, I was all about figuring out what I had to do and what I had to be for my kids. I went to work as a laborer doing whatever I could. Is that what I'm passionate about? No, but it's been good to show my kids that my failures don't define who I am today.

"Eventually, I got ahold of K.D., a guy who helped me lead some NA groups at STAR. I told him about my idea and said that I wanted him to be part of it. For several months, we tried to get together but just couldn't get our ducks in a row. Finally, I got him down there and we started RAW Addiction together. Then I brought in Aaron, which is probably the best thing I ever did. We've built a brotherhood together and have been back-to-back ever since. We started out on Saturday night at 9:00 because I wanted to reach people at a time when they might be out partying or not have a meeting to attend."

⊖ ⊖ ⊖

W hat I like about RAW Addiction is its homegrown authenticity. There's no big money behind it. If you've ever watched one of their Saturday night lives, you know how primitive the whole operation is. It's just a couple people sitting around a table talking about recovery. Yet, they have spawned imitation meetings among local treatment agencies and inspired other people to start their own weekly broadcasts. Whatever else you might say about this rag tag crew of former drug users, dealers, and their loved ones, they are doing something right.

John's vision for RAW is boundless. When I ask about the future, his eyes grow wide and he quickly remarks that what they've done so far is just the beginning. RAW Addiction: Through the Eyes of Recovery went live on Facebook for the first time in January of 2018, and they haven't missed a single Saturday since then. Even when the guys took a trip to New York City at the close of 2018, they went live from Times Square on New Year's Eve to show people you can still have fun when you're sober. Their consistency is impressive, and the loyalty they feel for each other comes out in every conversation I have with them. I also appreciate how accepting they are of different recovery paths. Even though their general approach is a departure from the anonymous tradition of AA and NA, they advocate for anything and everything that works.

In John's own words: "We're about change. We're about bringing people together in a community that has lost hope. I think there's a lot of people in Portsmouth, because of this epidemic, who would rather just go to work, come home, and lock their doors at night instead of being in the community. So, we're providing a stage for people to come out and speak their minds, whether they are addicts or if they are on the other side. That's why we started the loved ones group as well. Sometimes in addiction we forget about those who have it the worst—the husbands, wives, and children of those who are using. All of RAW Addiction is a family, though. When one gets down, the others will pick them up."

These are more than just words. In addition to their weekly social media broadcast, John and the others will often organize events for kids and people in need, like their annual coat drive and community Thanksgiving dinner. Last December, they even put on a play for the recovery community that a few of the guys wrote together when they were in the correctional facility. It was a spoof of Charles Dicken's classic holiday tale—"A Ghetto Christmas Carol!"

Currently, they're rehabbing an old house in one of Portsmouth's hardest-hit neighborhoods. Progress has been slow because money is tight, but John remains optimistic. Once the remodel is complete, they plan to turn it into a resource center for people in addiction. The message they are sending to the dealers next door is simple: "Either burn us out, join us, or leave."

John's confidence is inspiring, and I can easily tell why he's become a leader in the recovery community. He recognizes the wider problems we're facing as a society, but he believes the greatest barriers to recovery are individual and internal. Romans 12:2 is the basis of his philosophy. He read this verse for the first time while he was in the hole at Ross County, and it's stuck with him ever since.[4]

"Change the way you think, change the way you live," John says, his manner just as unassuming as when our conversation began. "That's

---

4   "Do not be conformed to this world, but be transformed by the renewal of your mind, that by testing you may discern what is the will of God, what is good and acceptable and perfect." (English Standard Version)

pretty much my story in a nutshell, and it's not over yet. There's still a lot of work to do."

Indeed, there is.

"YOU START USING, YOU LOSE EVERYTHING, AND YOU EITHER DIE OR GET BETTER."

Brooklyn's story challenges the theory that drug addiction is always the outcome of adverse childhood experiences and unresolved trauma. Perhaps her account is even more sobering for that reason. She invited me to her house one afternoon in the spring of 2019. As I recall, it was a bright and cheery day. When I arrived, I sat down at the kitchen table amidst photos of friends whom she has lost to drug overdose. As her son played and watched cartoons in the next room, Brooklyn opened up to me about her life.

"I grew up in the area," she begins. "Actually, just down the road from here in a house that's torn down now. I literally could not have asked for a better childhood. My mom has eleven brothers and sisters and my dad has four brothers, so I have a million cousins, aunts and uncles, and we're all very close. All good people. In school, I was always in sports and got good grades. I was prom queen. So was my sister. Actually, a lot of my cousins were, too," she chuckles. "It was kind of funny."

"So, in Minford there was this place called the Park-n-ride. It was a big hangout where people went after school and on the weekends. And I can remember in high school—this was right around the time when OxyContin came out. I didn't know what it was, though I'd heard people talk about it. But people would be standing at the Park-n-ride, pale as a ghost, eyes looking weird, and mid-conversation would just turn around and puke everywhere. I would get so mad, thinking, 'Why would you do that? Do you know how stupid you look?' But you know, when you're around something for so long, if your friends are doing it, you're going to do it. If there's an upside to it, I guess it's that I didn't try anything until I was out of high school. I eventually caved and did what they called a 'little' pain pill, which was like a Lorcet. It took me fifteen minutes to get up the nerve to snort it the first time.

"I did that several times until one night I was hanging out with a friend in Rosemount. He pulled out an OxyContin 80 and asked if me and my sister wanted some. We said yes and split it three ways. At first, I got really sick. I remember having to pull over on the side of the road and puke my guts out. But after I threw up, it was like every feeling I never had that I wanted—yeah, I had *that* feeling. It was amazing. Every time after you first get high, you're constantly chasing that feeling again, but you never get it.

"It took a while for things to get bad, though. At that point, I was eighteen. I still had an apartment and a roommate. I was going to college to be a teacher. I was having fun, thinking about what I wanted to be and what I wanted to do. But the next ten years—gosh, I could never put it all into words. I started skipping classes and blowing whatever student loan money I had left after school expenses on drugs. My car became the dope car. I was always on the road chasing dope.

"Even after I started using drugs, I was always the person everyone trusted. They knew I would never do 'em wrong, but, you know, you can only do drugs for so long and stay that way. Eventually, I was borrowing money and not paying it back and telling people I lost their money or that someone stole it. Or just flat out taking it from them. You've probably heard this, but I was the person who would steal your money and then help you look for it. I couldn't keep a job, either. In my early twenties I got fired from my job because I went to the bathroom and passed out for like thirty minutes. I tried to hide it from my mom, but she found out. That's when I think she first realized that I had a problem. It was devastating for her, of course. She went through that period of asking herself, 'Where did I go wrong? What could I have done differently?'

"But anything I could get my hands on at that point was fair game. I literally enrolled in school just because I knew I would get a couple thousand dollars in student loans. I didn't blow it all, but after the books and supplies for school were paid for, I was gone. I had tons of money but nothing to show for it. I made so many enemies during those days. I told you how big my family was. Well, there was maybe a handful left by the end who wanted anything to do with me. Even my mom. She's the type who will do anything for her kids, but even she got to the point where she had had it. She got to where she would let me stop by her house if I needed food or something, but other than that, I was on my own.

"Eventually, I didn't have a car or a phone and I was living at the end of this road," Brooklyn points out the window near where we are sitting, "in a deserted house that the government was taking for the bypass. My ex-boyfriend and I were literally sleeping on a dock-type thing at that pond up there. That's what my life had come to. My mom hated my boyfriend so bad that I would leave him there when

I went to shower and get some food at her house. As bad as it was, even while living in those conditions … all I cared about was having my drugs. I didn't want to be sick. I wanted to be high. But it was so surreal living like that because I had everything growing up. I had *the* best life you could ask for.

"Eventually, though, I decided I had enough. I was sick of hurting my mom. So, I went to a doctor and got on the Suboxone program. It worked and I was doing amazing. I got a job as a secretary and got back in school for real. But then one night, I was sitting here at home, minding my own business and doing homework," she points to a chair right behind where I'm sitting, "when the phone rang. It was midnight, so I immediately thought, 'This cannot be good.' Sure enough, it was a friend of mine who was at a house up the road from me. They needed a ride to Portsmouth because they were dope sick. And you know, I felt bad for them because I knew what it was like to be dope sick. My sister was with me and she said, 'Brooklyn, don't do it,' but I did. I picked them up and we went to Portsmouth. They got what they were getting, and stupid me, I ended up buying an Oxy-20, which I snorted.

"Well, we planned on going home a certain way, but then we saw a guy we knew out walking. It was cold, so I gave him a ride, and we ended up going the opposite way. That took us through a speed trap on 139. A state boy turned around and got me. Turns out I had an outstanding warrant for my arrest due to a bad check I'd written the year before. That's usually how it goes, you know. You're trying to straighten your life up, but your past starts catching up with you. You can't get away with it forever. That was 2007 and I was twenty-five years old. I had gotten away with it for about six or seven years before I got in trouble with the Law. So, because they had a warrant, I had to go to jail. They called my mom and woke her up at 2:00 in the morning to come and get the car. Mom and my sister show up and I'm in handcuffs … "

Brooklyn's voice cracks. Her eyes become red.

"My poor mom," she says. "She starts crying, begging the cops to take the cuffs off me. And me, that was the first Oxy I'd done in six months, so I was high. I'm like, 'Mom, they have to keep the cuffs on me, it's fine.' But the cops were kind of mean to her. They'd seen people like me so many times. This was the first time my mom had experienced anything like that, though. I ended up getting stuck in jail for eight days because there was a lapse in my paperwork, and, oh my gosh, even my friend who got arrested with me begged them, saying, 'Please, don't take Brooklyn back there. She won't survive. She won't make it!' She'd done been in jail once, so she knew what it was like. Somehow, her and the other guy ended up getting out that night, but I was stuck in there.

"So, I got put on misdemeanor probation. And everybody knows that probation and addiction do not mix. I was in and out multiple times until finally I caught a felony in 2010. It was a felony five for theft. I stole jewelry from a lady I was babysitting for and sold it. She pressed charges on me. It's funny now, though, because that same woman played a huge role in me getting off probation later on. She refused any of the restitution and wrote my probation officer a letter saying how proud she was of me and how happy she was to have the old Brooklyn back. She had been a friend of my family's for years.

"But now I was on probation for a misdemeanor *and* a felony. I was supposed to pay fines every month, but I didn't care about that; I wanted that money for drugs. Eventually, my probation officer got sick of my behavior and decided to lock me up. He would lock me up and let me out, lock me up and let me out. It got so bad, though. I stole thousands of dollars from my mother. I had completely broken her heart. I mean, I would literally army crawl through her bedroom when the lights were out to get the money in her purse."

Brooklyn falters at this point, searching for words.

"Even saying some of this stuff out loud sounds so weird to me," she says, shaking her head. "It's like, 'Are you serious, Brooklyn?' Like I said, though, I was in and out of jail so often. My parents would get so upset every time they let me out because they knew it was never enough to get me right. Actually, no amount of time in the county jail is enough to get anyone right, I'm here to tell you that. I didn't realize it until my third or fourth time, but there are so many drugs in jail. You wouldn't believe the stuff people bring in there—bags full of stuff.

"Anyway, I told you I had become a driver and my car was the dope car. Well, I'm not kidding. I literally knew every drug dealer in Scioto County, and everybody came to me. That's how I got mine. I would work out deals to get drugs in exchange for driving. That went on for a very long time, until I ripped off so many people that nobody wanted to deal with me anymore. It got to the point where my mom was getting phone calls and threats because of stupid stuff I had done.

"My family would take a trip to Myrtle Beach every year, which is one of my favorite memories from growing up. It's ironic, though, because the last hoorah before I went to prison was my family making that trip together. It was June 11-18 of 2011. I took enough pills with me to get by while we were there, and that was the week when the DEA started hitting all the pill mills and shutting them down. So, I came back from Myrtle Beach to *nothing*. I was freaking out. I called around and the only thing I could find was heroin, heroin, heroin. My brain wouldn't go there yet, though, and I was still on the hunt for my pills. At that point, I had never touched a needle and didn't plan on it. But a friend of mine called looking for heroin, and I told him I would try to find him some. Without thinking, just out of habit

I said, 'I'll go, but you gotta throw me some.' When we got there, though, I realized what I was doing and said, 'Wait a minute, what *is* heroin? Can I snort it?' Well, it was tar, so I couldn't snort it. But I'm so dope sick at this point that I'm sweating and puking. I was literally drenched in sweat. We went back to the house, and my friend offered to help. She wrapped one of those twirly car chargers around my arm and did it for me.

"Maybe you've heard people say that once you use a needle, you'll never go back to snorting or eating or whatever, that you're stuck. Well, that is very true. I still didn't know how to do it myself at that point, but I would go to a car wash and sit alone for an hour trying to get high with the needle. I learned real quick 'cause I had to. After I started doing heroin, though, oh my gosh." Brooklyn emphasizes those words "oh my gosh" with a foreboding tone. "Well, put it this way ... I started using heroin in June 2011, and by September of that year I was arrested and on my way to prison and not coming home."

Brooklyn was arrested after a botched attempt to rob her drug dealer. The situation was such a mess that Brooklyn's *mother* started receiving death threats because Brooklyn had used her cell phone during the robbery.

"Mom was frantic," Brooklyn says. "She came to my room—mind you, I'm thirty years old and still living with my mother at this point—to wake me up. She had already got in my purse and found five needles. She's like, 'Get up! I'm getting death threats. I'm calling the police to file a report.' I tried to convince her not to, but she was determined. I said, 'Mom, if the cops are going to come, I'm gonna leave because I'm on probation.' I knew I was dirty. But I found out really quick she wasn't calling to make a report, she was calling to turn me in. She was so scared someone was going to kill me or that I was gonna kill myself. When she woke me up, I was wearing my Myrtle

Beach t-shirt and I literally had blood all over my shirt where I was so high the night before and had missed trying to shoot up.

"The cop showed up and I freaked out. When he came to the door, he asked where the girl was he'd just seen on the porch. I was in my room, hiding. I heard Mom say, 'That's my daughter, Brooklyn,' and that's when I figured out she was turning me in. I had no choice but to come out. The officer asked for my probation officer's name and how long it had been since I reported. I was supposed to be reporting every week, but I hadn't called in for about five weeks. He told me he was gonna have to take me in, so I asked if I could brush my teeth and change clothes first. I didn't care about that, of course. I just wanted to go shoot the rest of my pills. I came back out looking the exact same as when I went in."

Brooklyn sighs. "I told myself I wasn't gonna cry," she says, then chuckles softly and lets out a long moan. "Ugh. Watching my mom watch me being taken away was horrible, though. She was devastated. Especially, I think, because she was the one who turned me in. But she had just had enough. I mean, it was either me in jail or me dead."

Brooklyn stands up and walks to the kitchen sink. I assume she needs a minute to collect her thoughts and let whatever she is feeling pass through her. She sets her cup on the counter and takes her seat again.

"Like I said," she continues, "I had been in jail before. I had gotten out every time, but I never took it as an opportunity to get better. When he pulled away with me in the car that night, though, I knew this was it. I knew I wasn't coming home for a while. As angry as I was—it was like I was angry at the world even though I knew it was my fault—I was also relieved." She lets out a long, exasperated sigh, evidently reliving the moment. "I mean, finally. Like, I was so sick of living like that. But when you're living like that, it's just so hard to see a way out.

"So, I went to jail for 109 days, and on December 28th, they came and got me for court. I had no idea I even had court. I thought I had another two or three months until my hearing. They had gotten me once before and offered me three years in prison, which I turned down. This time, the offer was two years in prison with a judicial out in six months to STAR. I'm in handcuffs and shackles, and I look over at my mom and dad. They're just devastated. My lawyer said, 'Just take it, Brooklyn. It's not gonna get any better.' Accepting that plea deal was the hardest thing I've ever had to do. Two years is a long time. Eventually, my mind started to clear, and I became grateful for the experience. I've always said that prison saved my life, and then STAR changed my life. I really learned so much about myself and about why I did the things I did. How to help other people and just how to live a normal life.

"I was gone for fifteen months altogether. I did 109 days in jail, seven months in Marysville, and 143 days in STAR. Coming home was a hard transition, but I was one of the lucky ones. My family supported me all the way through. At STAR, you started to earn passes to come home for a visit every so often. My first pass was right around Halloween, and I was so nervous. But it was great. Everyone kept calling because they heard I was home. Even still, the closer it came to the time for me to be released for good, I was so, so scared to go home. I knew I didn't want to go back to that life, but I was so scared that I was going to. Like, 'Who's gonna want to be my friend? Is my family going to accept me? Is anybody gonna trust me? Will I be able to get a job?' I had so many questions, the kind that anyone who's ever been locked up wonders about. I didn't know how it was going to be.

"When I came home, though, I wanted to be independent, so I started looking for a house. I found one, and within forty-five days I also had three jobs. The last one was at the Counseling Center. When they hired me, I quit the other two jobs and stayed there for two years. That was a huge, huge deal to me. I was so thankful to the ones who gave their time and energy during those fifteen months to help me get better that I wanted to do the same for other people. I always made sure my clients knew that they helped me just as much as I helped them. I met so many amazing people who just had a problem like I did.

"After leaving The Counseling Center, I worked at SOLACE until I became pregnant with my son, Jaxxon. Because I was high-risk, I decided it was best to stay home. Working in recovery is my absolute passion, but I've been so blessed to be able to work from home and be with him. He just started pre-school, so I'm finally considering going back to work again."

Brooklyn and I go on to talk about stigma, and she recalls the time a correction officer told her that all the drug offenders in prison (including her) should be taken out back and shot. We discuss the need for more treatment in lieu of conviction and how Brooklyn can't stand to hear people demean folks who use Suboxone to get better. And we talk about all the kids who've had to grow up in the middle of this crisis. If she had the money, Brooklyn would open "the biggest place you've ever seen" for kids to come and learn how valuable they really are.

As we approach the end of our conversation, I notice that Brooklyn's story has a "full circle" feeling to it. People take many different steps toward recovery, but for her, the overwhelming desire to get better for her family was enough. Her mom still feels guilty about what she could have done better as a parent; for this reason, Brooklyn has tried to identify some trauma or unresolved pain to explain why she became addicted to drugs. She can't find anything like that, though. The only explanation she can come up with is that she got in over her head while trying to have fun. For this reason, I suppose her story serves as a warning that what they say is true: *Addiction doesn't discriminate*. Certain folks may be predisposed to it in ways that others are not, but a person can have a happy childhood full of wonderful friends and family and still fall prey to the specter of substance use disorder.

Thankfully, Brooklyn's story has a happy ending. She ends it on the same note she began by talking about how good her life was and how good it is now.

"I know every person's story is different," she says. "But for people who use drugs, the cycle is basically the same: you start using, you lose everything, and you either die or get better. I'm just so glad I was one of the lucky ones. Like I said before, I had the best life growing up. Those ten or eleven years of addiction, I just threw away. I'm thankful for those years, although I do have a lot of regret for the people I hurt and the things I can't ever take back, but every single thing that happened got me right here."

She taps the surface of the table as if to let that point hang out between us for a moment. My attention is drawn to Jaxxon playing happily in the next room, where I hear his voice rising above the cartoons in the background. Brooklyn looks around and smiles.

"I own my own home," she says. "I have a beautiful son. I just bought a new car. I pay my bills without any child support, and my son has everything he wants. And even though I'm not currently in the treatment field, I still help people whenever they come to me. I try to stay as active as I can to help people who are using whether I'm in the field or not, because to me that's what recovery is all about. It doesn't matter where you work. My life's not perfect by any means, but to me, it's pretty darn close."

"THIS IS WHAT RECOVERY LOOKS LIKE: THE WHOLE COMMUNITY COMING TOGETHER."

I got to know Aaron while I was organizing for criminal justice reform during the 2018 mid-term elections in Ohio. He jumped right into that work and helped me build a bridge into the recovery community as a friend and ally. Since then, he has continued to develop himself both personally and professionally, and I've seen his passion carry through to the work he does in our local community. In many ways, I feel like the mutual respect Aaron and I have gained for each other is what made *The Face of Addiction* possible.

This is his story.

⊖ ⊖ ⊖

"I grew up in Rosemount and had a pretty good childhood," Aaron says. "My parents divorced when I was two years old. I was actually born in North Carolina, though my mother was originally from Portsmouth. I have two sisters and a brother, so I was the youngest of four growing up. My step-dad at the time—they were married from when I was four years old till about eleven—was verbally and physically abusive. But all in all I had a pretty decent childhood. Not terrible and not great at the same time.

"Rosemount was a good place to grow up. It was the type of place back then where you could leave your doors unlocked. I played a little soccer my freshman through junior year. I always kind of tended to run with the older kids. In school, I wasn't a great student. I did pretty much just enough to get by. I finished a little college at Columbus State where I went for one quarter for an Associate of Arts degree. However, I ended up meeting my ex-wife and she got pregnant shortly afterwards, so that kind of put a damper on things as far as my time for school." He chuckles. "Sometimes life doesn't care about your plans.

"When I was married to my ex-wife in Columbus around 1999, we both started using cocaine. That ended up causing a lot of problems in our marriage. We separated in 2003, and I moved back to Portsmouth. A big reason for that was me seeking a geographical cure—trying to get away from the cocaine use. So, I moved back down here and did pretty good for a few years. I got clean and started my own business, similar to what I was doing in Columbus, just a small remodeling company. Eventually, though, I started running around with some guys who were doing pain pills, like Vicodin and Percocet, and I started using those. Then I got a phone call from some guys in Columbus who were going to Florida for Oxycontin and Oxycodone. They had heard how much money you could make selling those down here, and they figured I would be a good connection to help them with it.

"So, I got involved with that. I sold them for a while before I started using them. At first, I wouldn't use them because I knew how addictive the Oxycontin was. But I was drinking one night, and I tried one and fell in love with it. From there, I started making trips to Florida myself and taking other people—sometimes three of four times a month. At least once a month I would go down, and if other people wanted to go, I would take them down with me. Basically, the deal was that if you paid for all the prescriptions and doctor visits, you could come back with about $8000 worth of pills. It was pretty lucrative," he pauses, "as long as you weren't using them constantly. That's how it started out when I wasn't using them as much. I had such a large amount on hand that there wasn't really any financial consequences to me using. So, me and my fiancé at the time, our tolerance got really high because we had access to pills pretty much all the time.

"But eventually they started cracking down on the Florida docs and stuff, so that came to an end. And here's me and my fiancé, both doing ten Oxy-30's a piece per day. Now we're at the point where we can't afford to do as much and that was probably the first time in three years where I knew what people meant by being dope sick. Everyone always talked about it and I thought they were exaggerating because I always had plentiful amounts, but when I started to experience that, well … "

Aaron sits back in his chair and groans. "They compare it a lot to the superflu," he says. "Just imagine constantly being on the toilet—you've got diarrhea, you can't really get comfortable when you're trying to sleep, your legs just keep moving. It feels like you've ran a marathon cause you're legs just keep moving and your muscles are so sore. It's just a horrible feeling. It lasted about four days for me. Actually, when I first experienced it, I thought, *Well, the first day wasn't too bad.* But then it seemed to progressively get worse as time went on until about the fourth day when I finally started feeling better. I was able to function, but it wasn't easy. I would still go to work, but I know a lot of people who couldn't."

Aaron's first real wake-up call came in Columbus in 2012 or 2013.

"Somewhere around that time, I was robbed at gunpoint," he says. "A 'friend' down in Scioto County knew I was dropping my kids off in Columbus. He said, 'Oh, I've got a friend up there who's got a really good deal.' Then the guy robbed me for $2,700. Just to show you where my mentality was at the time, though, consider this: when he pulled the gun on me, I said, 'You're not getting the money.' Then it was like a lightbulb went off in my head, and I thought, 'What are you doing? Are you serious? Are you really gonna get shot over $2,700?'"

He smiles incredulously, as if the whole thing seems ridiculous to him now.

"I ended up giving it to him. He got nervous and the gun started shaking so much that I thought he might shoot me on accident anyway. But that was an eye-opener for me, for sure. Even still, I felt like I was so far in at that point that I couldn't find my way out. My fiancé and I had talked about wanting to quit, trying to figure out how to quit, and we even decided a few times to quit selling stuff, but it seemed like every time we went to quit, someone would call me with this great, ridiculous deal or something. We talked about it, and it was like … this has got to be the devil. Every time I was ready to man up and beat this thing, something that seemed too good to be true would come along."

"At that point, my fiancé's dad, who is also an addict, told her that the best way to get off pain pills was to use crystal meth. I was totally against this idea, mainly because of my cocaine use. When my ex-wife and I were together, it had caused us so many problems that I knew speed was a really bad idea for a couple. I'd seen too many couples doing cocaine and meth together where bad stuff happened. Even though I was against it, I caught her using a few times behind my back, and I finally accepted the idea that if you can't beat em, join em. It did help me get off the pain pills, but now I had a whole new addiction.

"Since the Florida doctor thing was over, I had to find a new way to support my habit. So, I started getting boxes of Sudafed from the pharmacy. I'd go to Columbus once a week and pick up homeless people and pay them ten bucks a piece to buy a box of Sudafed, and I'd buy them a pack of cigarettes or whatever they wanted in return. Then I'd take the Sudafed to the guys who were making meth down here and they would give me $50 a box. I started bringing such a large amount that they would split the batch with me.

"Eventually, I started getting ripped off by those dealers. They would tell me, 'Oh, it didn't turn out the way it was supposed to,' and take advantage of me, so I went online and learned how to do it myself. Which I knew was a bad idea. I never actually wanted to learn, but I found out real quick that when you start making meth it becomes an addiction in itself. Just the process, you can't even explain it, but it really does."

Shades of Walter White, I think to myself, making an immediate connection to the television series, *Breaking Bad.*

"Then I came home one day—I wasn't home much at this point— and my son wasn't there. I asked my ex-wife where he was, and she said, 'My mom and dad came and got him and said we wouldn't get him back until we got off drugs.' I was livid. Of course, I'm blaming everything on her. 'Why would you let them take our son?' Looking back, though, it was probably the best thing they could have done. I didn't feel that way at the moment, obviously, but I knew I couldn't go to their house and start raising Cain, or else they would call the police and I definitely wouldn't get him back.

"Me and her split up shortly after that, and then I lost my house when my landlord had to move back into it. I really didn't have the means to go find something else, so I just started bouncing around from place to place. Then my buddy's mom, who had a house trailer that had been abandoned for a while, agreed to let me stay there. Basically, I just used it to go and cook. One night a guy asked me to help him cook up a batch, so we did. He had some people coming by because he was a heroin dealer, too, which I never messed with. But I was like, 'Why you got all these people coming by here?' so I left while he was finishing up.

"Well, I came back about an hour and a half later, and there were cops everywhere. They know my name already because the guy's girlfriend told them that everything was mine and that he was just watching the house for me. I became the fall guy, basically, and they arrested me. While we were in county jail fighting our case, that guy ended up overdosing—I assume it was on heroin—in the jail. His girlfriend dropped him off a pack. I remember vividly the morning he overdosed. The night before he had visitation—we were in separate tanks—and I could see him through the glass. He was so high. He was asking, 'Where's Lanier at?' while I was standing right in front of him. The next morning, after I ate breakfast and laid back down, I heard someone say, 'Two paramedics just went back with a gurney.' As soon as I heard that, I knew it was him.

"Seeing that happen made me realize the gravity of the situation I'd allowed myself to get into. After he died, my ex brought my son to visit me—my youngest son, Ryland, with whom I was really close—and just seeing how scared he was coming into that visitation room in the county jail made me feel helpless. I was supposed to be there to protect my kids, but when I saw how scared he was, I didn't even like him coming to the jail. It was really overwhelming for a four-year old kid. I basically felt like I was abandoning him. I had a moment of clarity where I began to see how many people I was hurting. The mentality of the addict is always 'Poor me—everyone's ganging up on me.' You always play the victim, but you don't see how much everyone else around you are the real victims.[5]

"At that point, around September 2015, I was looking at thirteen years in prison if I went to trial and lost. Since I wasn't there when they raided the place, it was questionable whether they could convict me or not. My daughter, who was seventeen at the time, came to visit me and was really upset. She said, 'I want you to be at my high school graduation.' At that point, she was going to be graduating in 18 months. That was upsetting. All my kids are close to me, but my daughter is daddy's girl.

"They offered me four years with judicial release in two years if I pled guilty, but I told them no. We ended up agreeing on four years with a judicial 'out' in one year where I would have to go to STAR. That deal put me out in 16 months, right before my daughter was set to graduate, so I took it. Even though I thought I might beat it if I went to trial, I wasn't going to take that gamble."

Aaron did his time in prison and then stepped down to STAR, the community-based correctional facility in Franklin Furnace, Ohio. That's where he met John Evans, the founder of RAW Addiction whose story appears in chapter six of this book. Before Aaron left for STAR, one of the guys in prison asked him to let John know that he was planning to return the bible John had loaned to him.

---

5 Moments like these often become turning points for people in recovery. Seeing the negative impact of their actions on people they love can provide the motivation they need to change. For more on the concept of human connection being the catalyst to overcome addiction, check out Johann Hari's TED talk, "Everything you think you know about addiction is wrong," or better yet, read his book, *Chasing the Scream*.

"The way John carried himself was different than a lot of the guys," Aaron says. "He didn't have that macho, gotta-be-hard attitude. You could tell he'd really worked on himself and changed his whole mentality. Even still, I was skeptical at first and wondered if he was genuine or if it was just "fake it to make it," as they say in treatment. But as time went on, I saw that he was serious about the things he said and what he was doing. At the time, he had some good ideas but didn't know how they were going to turn out yet.

"So, I got out of STAR, but then I relapsed about a week before John went live with his first RAW Addiction video. When I commented on the livestream, John invited me to come on with him the following week. I believe it was the fourth video when I finally went on and told my story, and I just kept going with it from there."

⊖ ⊖ ⊖

My respect for Aaron has only grown since I've known him. We ended our conversation by talking about the importance of choosing our response to life's circumstances. Looking back, I recall the decision Aaron made to stop using drugs when he realized how it was hurting his son. What a difference that choice made between life and death. Had he chosen otherwise it very well could have been him who was carried out on the gurney that day.

Instead, Aaron's entire life has changed, affirming the truth of Robert Frost's iconic line: "Two roads diverged in a wood, and I—I took the one less traveled by—and that has made all the difference." Since our interview, Aaron has completed probation, obtained his Chemical Dependency Counselor Assistant (CDCA) license, and has started working at Port 45, a treatment agency located in Portsmouth, Ohio. He believes the tide is slowing turning in the opioid epidemic due to the fact that so many kids are against drugs now, having seen firsthand the devastation in their parents' lives. While he's glad to be working at "ground zero" in Scioto County where so many people come from across the state for treatment, he's convinced that we need more options for people in recovery—things like SMART Recovery and Life Ring, just to name a few. Such alternatives are hard to come by in a culture that is steeped in the conventional 12-step approach.

"What drives me more than anything, though, is being a positive role model," he says. "Just to set an example for other people in the community who have struggled with the same things I've struggled with. I want to be the exception. To show people that your life can change, even though it may take some trials and tribulations. I spent a lot of time being part of the problem as an addict and a dealer, so I still live with a lot of guilt for playing my part in people's suffering. Now, I want to not just change myself but change the community to create a better future for our children. This is what true recovery looks like: the whole community coming together to fight this epidemic. There is strength in numbers. If we all work together, our community will overcome this!"

"IF YOU NEED HELP, IT'S HERE."

Elizabeth's story is unique for the way it highlights the devastating intersection between substance use disorder and gender dysphoria. The LGBTQ community is especially vulnerable to a host of debilitating issues that often lead people into drug addiction. Elizabeth is no stranger this tale, so I was eager to hear what she had to say. We sat down together outside the coffee shop in Portsmouth, Ohio, one sunny afternoon in April 2019. Over the din of passing cars, she told me her story.

⊖ ⊖ ⊖

"I grew up in Stout, real close to Shawnee Forest. Mom is from Kentucky, Dad's from around here. I definitely had that Bible belt, fundamentalist Christian upbringing. Things were great for years. I didn't really question my beliefs until I got a little older and started to realize that I was attracted to men."

The significance here is that Elizabeth grew up as a boy.

"Of course, my church was very much against homosexuality," she explains. "Yet, I also identified as a Christian. I was raised in church and very involved in my congregation. I did the church plays, Vacation Bible School—all that jazz. I was even trained to be a church pianist. But when I began to realize I was attracted to men, things changed. I started to feel unwelcome at church. No one said anything to me in particular, but all the sermons about being gay and how that was a sin began to weigh on me."

Elizabeth sighs, evidently struggling to find words. "Even still, everything was ok until I came out to my mom. I was fourteen at the time. I just kind of said, out of the blue, 'Mom, I'm gay,' while fighting with her. She told my dad, and he didn't talk to me for about a week. They both ended up sitting me down not long after that, though. They opened their Bibles and read to me and told me I was an abomination."

The weight of this memory hangs in the air between us for a moment. I say nothing, waiting for Elizabeth to continue.

"My mom was very emotionally unstable growing up. Very emotionally unavailable." She emphasizes the word "unavailable" in a way that I can feel what it must mean for her. "My dad wasn't around because he was in the Air Force, so I didn't really have a steady family life growing up. I always had food, I had a roof over my head and clothes on my body—I never needed anything physically—but emotionally, it was very lacking.

"Then, it was during middle school—even though I didn't have the words to express it and didn't even know it was a thing—when I began to experience gender dysphoria. I was unhappy with my body, I was unhappy with my voice … I just thought I was being a typical middle schooler. Some of that feeling is normal at that age, but beyond the general body dysmorphia, I was also experiencing gender dysphoria. I didn't *like* being a boy. I thought if I prayed enough, it would all go away. But it never did."

According to the New Oxford American Dictionary, gender dysphoria is "the condition of feeling one's emotional and psychological identity as male or female to be opposite to one's biological sex." In other words, when a person experiences gender dysphoria, their body is saying one thing while their brain is saying something else. In Elizabeth's experience, this worked itself out in the form of acute psychological distress and anxiety-ridden panic attacks. Desperate for relief from the mental agony, she would physically harm herself to escape the feelings of dysphoria and to "bring herself back" from states of disassociation.

She continues, "So, you know, I had this history of self-abuse and trauma. Then I went to a graduation party in high school—I was seventeen—where people were drinking. Whenever I got drunk, I liked it, because it was an escape from my reality. I continued drinking as a way to cope when I went to college, where I also began smoking weed. From there, it just kind of progressed."

Other elements play into Elizabeth's story of substance abuse at this point. Her dad had been diagnosed with cancer before she left high school but had gone into remission twice. The family thought he had beaten it, but during her sophomore year of college they got the bad news: Elizabeth's dad was dying.

"I withdrew from school," she says. "That entire time was a blur. I don't think I was sober for one minute of it. But after Dad died, I was determined to go back. I thought it was what he would want. So, in January 2016, less than three months after he passed away, I re-enrolled in class. I don't know how I did it, but I did.

"Later that year, I got into harder drugs for the first time. Pills, LSD, coke—whatever I could find. Life became a chase for the next, biggest high. I ended up having to withdraw the next semester, though, because I was diagnosed with vocal nodules. As a singer, that's very debilitating. I dropped out of class and spent the next few months just floating around Athens, working and using and running out my lease. I attempted suicide at that point. I ran into traffic and got hit but came out of it with just a sprained ankle and a contusion on my arm. I was lucky.

"When my lease ran out, I moved back to Scioto County with my mom. At first, I thought I would just go back to work, but the suicidal thoughts persisted. Finally I just said, 'Mom, I need to go get help.' So, I was hospitalized for about a week. When I got out, I was taking such a heavy cocktail of medication. They gave me, essentially, chemical restraints. It was literally a laundry list of all these psychosomatic medications." She laughs nervously. "I would wake up in the morning and I still wouldn't feel awake until like an hour and a half after I'd woken up."

Elizabeth was still using drugs when she was hospitalized in May 2017. Her mom knew about the marijuana but not "the other stuff." After hearing about a rehab in Michigan from one of her co-workers, Elizabeth's mom brought up the possibility of treatment. This particular facility had a special program for weaning people off their depression and anxiety meds along with any illegal substances they were using.

"That's the best thing my mom has ever done for me," Elizabeth says. "I'll still give her props for this … She gave me the *choice*. She didn't say, 'You're going there, and that's that.' She said, 'You can go here if you want.' And I went. I was in-patient for a month and a half. After that, I went to a sober living facility in Los Angeles. By then, it was July and I missed home. I missed Appalachia. I know a lot of people encourage others to get out of here, but I don't want to leave. I want to work in this area because it needs help."

I mention how strange that might sound to other people in Elizabeth's position, but she laughs and says, "I don't want to go somewhere and have it easy. I'm a little bit of a masochist in that aspect. But I really do want to help people. There are a lot of LGBTQ people in Appalachia who are really struggling because of the stigmas about them."

Of course, she's not joking on this point. I recall being told about a certain local church whose denominational affiliation would suggest a welcoming stance toward sexual minority groups. Years ago, however, a same-sex couple moved to town and sent a letter to the church asking if it would be alright for them to attend service on Sundays. The church council president was kind enough to write them back and tell them they weren't welcome. Not even to come to church. Welcome to Appalachia.

"But back to the story," Elizabeth says. "I decided to come home because the cost of living in California is terrible, and I had completely depleted all my savings. At that point, I had been sober for about three months, and I was dumb. I thought I was good, so I started working as a bartender. And for a while; a few weeks, I was fine. People would ask me to have a drink with them and I'd say 'Sorry, I can't,' and flash them a chip. But then, of course, the addict in me rationalized, and I started drinking again. Then one night while I was drunk, someone offered me crystal meth. Honestly, from August to January after that, everything is a blur."

I can sense the pain Elizabeth still feels while thinking about that time. "I kind of don't want to remember it," she says. "I acknowledge it, because it got me where I am now, but it was a really terrible time. Everything was going wrong. I got into sex work to finance my drug use and spent most of my time smoking meth, until finally I had a moment of clarity, and I asked one of my friends for help. She told me about a friend of hers who worked at a rehab in Portsmouth, and she was able to get me in. They helped me get clean, this time for good.

"A few months later, though, some other issues re-surfaced. In February, I started feeling really anxious. I had explored my gender identity in Los Angeles and while I was in-patient in Michigan. I self-identified as gender fluid at that time. But when I got home, I didn't feel like I could do that. I was living with my mom and she would not have that whatsoever. Plus, it was Appalachia. I didn't think it was possible to be trans in Appalachia. Eventually, though, I confided in my therapist. I said, 'I think I'm trans. No—I *know* I'm trans.' She helped me transition."

I'm curious to hear about the transition process but don't know if I should ask about it. Elizabeth continues without prompting: "You have to jump through so many hoops just to transition. Medically, socially … it's expensive. It's a lot." She emphasizes the word "lot" and then sighs. "But, I'm happy now. I've been able to stay clean since then. After a while, I exhausted the rehab's financing options and couldn't stay there any longer, but I found a support group at the Portsmouth Welcoming Community and began going to Cincinnati Children's Hospital for additional transition care."

Children's Hospital is where Elizabeth found out—surprise, surprise—that her vocal nodules had been a misdiagnosis.

"That was so relieving," she says, "because I thought all my hopes and dreams had been dashed. It was really nice to hear that I had a chance after all. I applied back to school, which was also like jumping through a million hoops just to get my scholarships back since my mom had kicked me out of the house when I came out as trans. That was in March 2018. I was three months sober when she kicked me out. But I survived homelessness. I stayed sober that entire time because I had friends I could stay with. They supported me and helped me get where I am now. I finally got my own place in Portsmouth a year later. In January, I auditioned for the School of Music and passed. I applied for a national LGBTQ scholarship that works with people who want to help the LGBTQ community in their own hometowns. Out of 2,100 applicants, only me and fifteen other people were picked."

Sadly, Elizabeth's relationship with her mom is strained now.

"We don't talk a lot," she says. "I don't feel comfortable seeing her anymore. We had this back-and-forth thing where we would talk with each other and fight, and then talk with each other and fight. Finally, I said, 'I can't do this anymore. I can't keep going in circles.' Mom's just very conflicted. She obviously loves me. I'm her child. But she still sees me as her son, and she refuses to see me as her daughter. She won't budge on that. She thinks my transition is against her religion. And it's been so detrimental to my mental health to try to get her to budge that I finally had to move on. I said, 'If you're not going to stand with me, then bye.' My mental health has been a lot better since then. Our back-and-forth was just so toxic."

"What was it like with her before you came out as trans?" I ask.

"Well, she was ok with me being gay," Elizabeth says, "even though she wasn't really. It's just that being gay was a lot easier to overlook than being trans. Being gay isn't exactly as visible," she laughs nervously. "I mean, if you have a boyfriend and you want to bring him around, that's visible. But being trans is a very visible change, and I think that's what caused a lot of issues with her."

And her dad?

"Dad passed when I was still living as a gay man. He never came out and said, 'It's ok that you're gay.' But before he died, in some of his last moments of lucidity, he told me how much he loved me and how much he would always love me." She pauses thoughtfully. "I could see that he was very upset over how he had acted. He acted very aggressive when I first came out. Very distant.

"I actually dream about him now," she continues. "A couple times in my dreams he has told me he's ok with my transition. Actually, in my last dream—when I was struggling with separating from my mom—she and dad were divorced in the dream because he wanted to support me and she didn't. You know, maybe that's my own sub-conscious making a healing fantasy, but even if so, I'll take it!" she laughs heartily. "I'll take it and run with it. Actually—this is a little embarrassing, but I'll share it with you—I often have conversations with him. Almost every morning on my way home from work, I talk to my dad. It's weird how much it helps."

Her voice cracks as she repeats, "It's *so* helpful."

Elizabeth understands her own addiction primarily as a means of escape. "I was trying to escape the trauma of having an emotionally unavailable mother and a physically absent father," she explains. "I was also trying to escape the trauma of gender identity dysphoria, which is big in itself. Gender dysphoria is like living in a constant state of panic, thinking, 'Something is wrong.'"

She explains the underlying phenomenon of transgender people—identifying with a gender that is opposite one's biological sex—in very simple terms: "I was born with the body of a boy, but I have the brain of a girl." She cites some of the latest scientific research to corroborate her experience.[6]

And Christianity? "I believe in the teachings of Jesus," she says, "but I don't believe in the teachings of the church. Not any church in particular but historic, fundamentalist Christianity. Even some non-literalists can still be pretty fundamentalist." Elizabeth resonates most with the principles of Unitarian Universalism, but she still feels overwhelmed when someone pulls out a Bible because it reminds her of that horrible meeting with her parents. In fact, the last time she

---

6   Check out Amy Ellis Nutt's book *Becoming Nicole* for more information.

attended a Palm Sunday church service, she had to leave the building with a panic attack.

Despite the unique struggles she continues to face, however, Elizabeth is looking forward to the future. Since our interview, she has traveled to California and won the LGBTQ scholarship. She is enrolled at Ohio University in Athens again and has remained abstinent from drugs. She still has a ways to go on her degree, but she wants her life to count toward helping people both in and out of the LGBTQ community who wrestle with substance use disorder. Music therapy is her jam, and although it can help people with any number of developmental issues, she can't escape the glaring overlap that exists between SUD and sexual minority groups.

"Many LGBTQ people, especially in Appalachia—their lives are filled with guilt and shame and trauma. This is coming from their families, their friends, their churches, their schools, and their work. You can't escape the stigma in Appalachia, but a lot of them try to escape it with drugs. I mean, back when I was using, it wasn't hard for me to go on Grindr and find a guy doing meth. It's very prevalent in the gay community across the Tri-State."

Even when Elizabeth was in the behavioral unit after attempting suicide, she would play the piano and sing for her fellow patients. "I did that a lot for myself but also for them," she explains. "I could see a spark of hope in their eyes just by paying attention to them and learning more about them through the music. Recovering addicts, too—it's like it helped them find hope."

Coming to the end of our conversation, I feel confident that whatever Elizabeth ends up doing with her degree, her message will be the same. As a final note, I ask what she would say to someone who is reading this book and facing challenges similar to her own.

She thinks for a moment and then answers softly, "I'm here for you. I will not shame you. If you need help, it's here."

"FOR THE FIRST TIME, I AM COMFORTABLE IN MY OWN SKIN."

I've known Denice for a couple of years. Her quirky, lighthearted personality never fails to make me smile. She's the kind of person who can find something to laugh about in even the most painful situations. If I had to guess, though, I'd say that Denice is just like the rest of us in that her strengths can also be her weaknesses. Underneath her playful demeanor lies a world of hurt, and I get the impression she sometimes uses that playfulness as a way of masking the pain she feels inside. Of course, this just makes her human. We all do it.

Pain, however, is what often drives a person to addiction. Whether it's the pain of physical injury that leads to chemical dependency on prescription medication or the overwhelming distress of unresolved psychological trauma, unhealed wounds can easily become the source of addictive patterns. This is why the Canadian physician Dr. Gabor Maté says it is important to always ask, "not 'why the addiction,' but 'why the pain.'"

Either way, I appreciate the candor with which Denice approached our conversation. I began with a simple lead: "When did addiction start for you?" She responded with a straightforward answer: "Well, that goes back to birth."

⊖ ⊖ ⊖

"As a teenager, we just called it 'having fun.' I was married in 1978, but was told I couldn't have children. My husband and I raced cars and drank a lot of beer. The cocaine followed. It just kind of went hand-in-hand with what we were doing. All my friends were having kids, and I couldn't, and it was 'poor me.'"

She pauses, then looks at me mischievously. "As in, 'Pour me another one.'"

"Well, fifteen years later, I actually did get pregnant with my first child. I read all the books and tried to do everything right. Five and a half years later, I got pregnant with my second child. She arrived two months early and came home on oxygen with apnea. She was only four pounds when I brought her home.

"One day, my husband sent me out with my friend since I hadn't been out of the house in a while. While I was gone, he unplugged her. I mean, he knew she would be alright; he wasn't deliberately trying to harm her. But since the doctor hadn't told me it was ok to take her off the machine, I felt betrayed. I came home drunk and was like, 'You promised me you would take care of her, but you unplugged her machines!' That was the beginning of the end for us. When she was about eighteen months old, I left him. I moved out on my own and began raising the kids. He got partial custody every other weekend, so I started partying every other weekend when my kids were gone. And, well, it progressed.

"At first I told myself, 'It will never be in the house when the kids are home.' Well, that didn't last very long. They began to notice the change in me. I'd get them up for school, but then I would lay on the couch all day until they came home. Then I would stay up all night using cocaine. Finally, my oldest daughter, who was going into her freshman year of high school, came to me and said, 'Look, Mom, I know you're on drugs. Something's got to give.' I remember confessing to my eleven-year-old that mommy was on drugs. She had this one tear come out, and it looked *huge*. Oh, it was so awful."

She sighs, then shrugs her shoulders and smiles. "But I went to treatment."

Denice's first experience in treatment was at Stepping Stones in Portsmouth, Ohio, where she was introduced to the message of Narcotics Anonymous. She helped start a program for people in the county jail and even dreamed of starting her own house one day.

"It was great because I was all about it," she explains. "I bought into everything. I didn't realize that some women were there just to get their kids back. I thought everyone genuinely wanted help. But I ate, drank, and slept NA."

Then, she relapsed.

"I was at my daughter's graduation party, and I thought I could drink and get away with it because, you know, alcohol wasn't my problem. I drank alcohol a lot when me and my husband were racing, but when I started using cocaine, I had quit drinking. And I thought that everything I learned in the program only applied to my 'drug of choice.' Of course, they say alcohol is a drug, but after four years I had twisted it in my mind. Somehow, the disease talked to me and said, 'You can drink.' Well, no I can't.

"At that point, my husband and I had started seeing each other again, trying to put our family back together. We weren't living together, but we were on good terms. He had a place on the river where we went camping with our friends one week. And we drank. A *lot*. That was the summer of 2006."

Denice and her husband had a jet ski with them that weekend. One of their friends wanted to ride it, drunk, and even though they refused, he jumped on anyway. On his way back across the river, he tried to splash them, but when he slung the tail end of the machine around, he struck Denice in the face and knocked her unconscious. The men scrambled to pull her out of the water and performed CPR. By the time the rescue helicopter landed in her back yard, Denice says, she had already learned quite the lesson that day.

"Don't drink and jet ski," she says matter-of-factly, then busts out laughing.

Of course, it was more serious than that. They life-flighted Denice to Cabell Hospital in Huntington, West Virginia. On the way there, her brain swelled so much that they didn't think she was going to make it. Thankfully, her story wasn't over yet.

"They did an amazing job," she says. "I'm blind in my right eye and I have a few scars, but not as many as I might have. Most people say they can't tell, but they reconstructed the whole right side of my face. My husband and kids stayed with me while I was in intensive care. When I asked my daughter if I was going to die, she just said, 'No, but you won't have to buy two contact lenses anymore.' That's when I knew I was at least going to be ok. It took several surgeries to repair the damage to my face, though.

"They released me with OxyContin. 20 milligrams. I had to go back for two or three more surgeries, and each time I went they upped my dosage. By the time they were finished, I was getting 80 milligrams for the pain and 30 milligrams for what they called 'breakthrough' pain, which was in case additional shards of fiberglass they might have missed started seeping out of my eye."

"Did the doctors warn you about how addictive OxyContin could be?" I ask.

"No," she shakes her head emphatically, "they didn't say anything! They told me they had a new drug, that's all. They didn't tell me it was addictive. But I knew from the feeling right away. I knew when I *needed* to take it. My kids and my husband noticed, too. I kept needing more, but I used every excuse in the book for why my need was legitimate." She sighs. "But finally, I listened.

"I went back into treatment, and coming off of OxyContin was the worst thing ever. Oh my gosh. I don't know about heroin, but with Oxy I was sick, throwing up, going to the bathroom ... my whole body ached. Even my bones hurt. Especially my face. The nerve endings in there were wanting that pill! The withdrawal symptoms lasted about five days, but my body kept craving it a lot longer than that. Every ache or pain I ever had as a child came back and said, 'Feed me!'"

The next stop on Denice's road to recovery was at St. Lucy's. Just like her first time in treatment, she dove headlong into Narcotics Anonymous.

"And it worked," she says, laughing, "for another five years. This disease will convince you of all kinds of things. I don't think I was convinced that I was an addict at that point—I just liked to get high. But I'm totally convinced now. There's no ifs, ands, or buts."

Surprisingly, Denice shifts the conversation to medication-assisted treatment, or MAT for short.

"Before, you know, I was totally against Suboxone. That's about when Suboxone, Methadone, and the other treatments first came out. But what NA teaches us is that we're going to get clean and lead a productive life. So, if you can lead a productive life with Suboxone or whatever it takes, then I'm all for it. Of course, NA doesn't agree with that."

Narcotics Anonymous was founded on the model of its predecessor, Alcoholics Anonymous, which teaches a strict, abstinence-only approach to any kind of substance. Proponents of NA believe that depending on medication assistance is just "swapping one drug for another," or in other words, that it's not real recovery.

Despite her early devotion to this philosophy and her respect for those for whom it works, abstinence isn't a universal rule for Denice anymore. Now, she sees abstinence as more of a personal choice which someone like herself may have to make out of necessity. "If you can have a drink or a glass of wine, then so be it," she says. "But I know I can't do that if I want to stay in control." In addition to her personal experience, Denice has observed that the abstinence-only approach doesn't have a high success rate for long-term recovery. In fact, she estimates that only 3 out of 10 people actually "make it" on the abstinence-only track.

What happens when people who place all their trust in abstinence do relapse? "It is so, so shameful," Denice says. "It was so hard for me to walk back in those rooms and admit, once again, that I'm a failure. My views on MAT began to change when I saw it working. When I worked at SOLACE, for instance, I saw women getting jobs, going to meetings, and getting their kids back. Their lives were better." She raises her hands with both palms upturned in a sign of resignation. "So what if they were getting help?"

According to Denice, the majority view in the recovery community throughout southern Ohio is that medications like Suboxone are a crutch. Despite the negative view of MAT that still prevails throughout the county, however, she does see the narrative shifting. She names specific people in the community whose views have changed along with her own. Much of this change is due to the overdose crisis.

"They say you don't have clean time until you're off Suboxone. They are very adamant about that. But like I said, the program teaches us to become productive members of society—however you can do that. We've just had so many deaths. I would rather people be on something and be able to maintain than to be in a grave. Something is better than nothing."

The same goes for harm reduction.

"Some people say you shouldn't carry Naloxone,"[7] she says, "but if I had cancer, would you not give me medication? Naloxone saved my daughter's life. And she is now a very productive member of society. She has a family, a home, and she doesn't do drugs. That was just a portion of her life, you know. Had they not had NARCAN®, I'd be visiting her grave site."

Faith has played a big role in Denice's recovery as well. In fact, the first place I ever met Denice was at church. She has nothing but praise for the members of Christians Beyond Church, a small congregation on Highland Avenue in Portsmouth, Ohio, and she loves to tell the story of her first visit.

"I had used drugs the night before," she says. "At that point, I was shooting up. I hit a vein and registered blood. But I was done with life that night. I tried to push the needle in and kill myself—what they call a hotshot. But it wouldn't go in. So, I registered again. Blood came out and I pushed, but it wouldn't go in. I tried a third time, and when it didn't go in again, I said, 'I hear you, God.'"

An old song came to her mind: "Where can I go but to the Lord?"

"I dropped the needle and got on my knees. The next morning was Sunday, so I got my tennis shoes and put on my little dress and took off looking for a church. That's when I found Christians Beyond Church. The welcome sign was just waving at me, saying 'Over here, over here!'" she laughs. "I only knew two people there that day, but everyone welcomed me with open arms."

---

7   Naloxone, better known for its common brand name NARCAN® is the life-saving opiate overdose reversal drug.

I smile because I've heard this story before. Denice goes on and on about how much the congregation has cared for her since she first walked through the doors seven years ago. She joined a small group and started taking vacations with some of the other women. "I don't know what I'd do without my ladies," she says. "The support they've given me has helped me draw closer to God. Some of them might say I've grown up, but I've also gotten on some psych meds, and that helps."

She chuckles and flashes that mischievous grin again.

"Some people in recovery don't agree with psych medication either," she says. "But I need it. And I'm comfortable in my own skin now. Before, I would self-medicate a lot because the ups and downs were just too much to handle. But now with what they have me on, I'm ok. I can sit here and not be bouncing off the walls with nervous energy."

I realize that what's she's telling me is true. The Denice I've always known could hardly sit still for more than a few minutes, let alone endure a full interview without pulling at her hair the entire time. Sitting across the desk from me now, though, she appears to be relatively at ease, as if she is more present in the moment. I mention this fact and she smiles. Then I notice the clock on the wall behind her and realize that our time is almost up.

"In light of all the changes in your life," I ask, "how do you feel about the progress you've made so far?"

"Oh, I think I'm a success," she responds. "Without God, though, I would be nothing." She laughs as if she enjoys hearing herself say that, and I laugh with her. It's the kind of laugh you might hear at the end of a long-fought battle. Of course, Denice's battle isn't over yet. Anyone in recovery will tell you that it's a day-to-day thing. You get out of bed, you make the right choices, you don't pick up, and you live your life. But you need something more to motivate you than just the imperative to "stay clean."

Denice embodies this truth. Yeah, she's a recovering drug user, but she is so much more than just that. She's a wife, a mom, and a grandma, and right now her greatest motivation in life is to see her grandbabies grow up and flourish. The youngest is just getting ready to turn one, and he is more than enough reason for her to leave that needle in the past.

"I JUST WANT US TO MOVE ON... LIKE IT WAS A BAD NIGHTMARE."

There are some people in recovery who feel the need to remain anonymous, either to maintain the tradition they learned from Alcoholics and Narcotics Anonymous or for more practical reasons known only to themselves. Sometimes their family or social situation is too delicate and it's simply not enough to change the names of the people involved in their story. That's the case in this chapter. Jeanne wanted to share a brief account of her experience, strength, and hope, but she also had people to look out for. Her name is not Jeanne, but this is her story.

⊖ ⊖ ⊖

"I was allowed to start drinking when I was fourteen," she begins. "My parents were divorced when I was four. That's relevant because at fourteen I was drinking with both parents' knowledge and consent. Family outings on my mom's side—we went on beach trips and things like that—all revolved around drinking. We had our own beer cooler, and everyone got drunk. I started smoking cigarettes around the same time.

"When I came home during the summers and holidays, my dad's house was a party house. After Friday night football games, everyone came to his house and partied. He would go out and stay gone all night, so if something bad happened, he wouldn't be liable because he didn't know.

"As a senior in high school, I drank with my mom, even on school nights. I was eighteen but everyone thought I was twenty-one; they didn't really card. Halfway through my senior year, I moved home with my dad and did the same thing there."

Jeanne sighs. "So many things," she says. "I'm gonna try to leave some of it out." I nod, and she continues.

"So, I struggled with drinking my whole life. My cousin died when I was in high school and that was a big turning point for me. I turned to drinking more to cope with my loss. Then, when I moved back home, it got really bad. I didn't get sober until I was twenty-six. The point is, it was always socially acceptable in my family to drink. It's just what we did. It was like a cultural thing that led to my alcoholism."

There were other factors, too.

"I had severe depression as a child," Jeanne continues. "I didn't realize this until I was older. God revealed it to me when I was about thirty-one. I actually still struggle with it. I have social anxiety as well. I've gotten better with it because I'm more comfortable with who I am now, but I think that's a lot of what was behind my drinking. I would drink so I wouldn't have to feel or think. My mind never stops—I'm an empath—so the drinking helped numb that experience.

"I didn't realize the depth of addiction in my family until I got older. There are alcoholics on my mom's side. On my dad's side, there's just a long list of drug dealers. I found out that my grandma and grandpa on my dad's side had my cousin selling pills at fourteen when the opiate epidemic first hit. They even had my brother selling when he was in high school; that's how his addiction began. I was in a different state, so I didn't know about it at the time. My other cousin was also selling in high school and I had no idea. All this has just come out in the past year. Looking at it now," she says, "I see that not a single grandson on my dad's side has amounted to anything. All of them have been in jail or prison. I recently decided to cut my brothers out of my life for this reason. They love their ways, but it's not something I want for my kids."

The lines on Jeanne's face tense. I can tell the weight of these revelations are weighing heavily on her.

"I came to my sobriety through Christ," she says. "He walked me through the twelve steps before I even knew what they were. God literally saved my life from destruction. Time after time, God has shown up in my life. Mom taught me the basics of faith when I was young. She taught me things like, 'If you have faith the size of a mustard seed, God will move mountains for you.' I've held onto that, and I know it's what saved me.

"Now, I'm here to break generational curses in my family. The curse of alcoholism and drug addiction … Those things will not pass on to my children." She pauses, then repeats herself. "They will not pass on."

"How has your decision to cut ties with your wider family affected your kids?" I ask.

"Well, my daughter's dad died of an overdose when she was eleven," she replies. "It's been brought to my attention recently that he was a narc, and two people have told me they gave him a hotshot.[8] My daughter doesn't know that. She never met him. I also recently discovered that my daughter used to look up to my brother, who is currently in rehab, as a father. She's been in counseling for a while. Lots of anxiety and stress.

---

8 A "hotshot" is when a person intentionally injects enough drugs to kill themselves or someone else.

"My son … I've really tried to shelter and keep him away from it all. I've had to tell my mom that I don't want them at my house anymore. I'm getting ready to have that talk with my dad again, too, because he would bring my brothers to my house even when they weren't supposed to. So, I'm having to reset boundaries again. And again, and again."

Codependency doesn't seem to be an issue with Jeanne. "Because I was an alcoholic, I've learned how to not enable," she says. "God has helped me learn this, and I've also learned it through various classes and just being part of that community. Boundaries aren't hard for me to set. I don't have a problem with cutting anyone out of my life.

"You have to be able to do it. Towards the end, I think my dad may have been more involved in the drugs and possibly had my brother selling them, too. My parents have been divorced thirty-some years and my mom hates my dad. Everyone comes to my house for the holidays, including mom and dad, and now she won't even speak to him. I've watched Dad's health deteriorate over the past year and a half because of all the abuse. His parents are gone now, and thank God they are, because even though I wouldn't want to have to be the one to turn them in, I would. I asked Dad about him selling, but he denied it. He'll deny it till the day he dies. And my mom—it's just taking my mom. She doesn't use drugs herself, but that's still what it does. Addiction takes the whole family down with it. It takes down everything around you. And that's the hardest part … my mom."

Jeanne pauses. Her voice becomes soft.

"Mom and I were best friends. Now, every time I see her, the pain is just written all over her face. Her expressions used to be so gentle, so kind. Now, they exude anger, pain, frustration, and despair. Her heart is broken. She feels like she's failed at the most important job there is—being a mother."

Some of the information Jeanne shared with me during our inter-view she later asked me to remove from the story. I respect her desire to protect her family, and I appreciate the sensitivity she shows toward the people who have brought her so much grief. At the end of our con-versation, she finally circles back to my question about her children.

"With the kids," she says, "we just don't speak about it around them. I just want us to move on like it never happened ... like it was a bad nightmare."

Something in me recoils from this statement at first, but then I realize that this is where Jeanne finds herself right now. This is what she needs to do to survive and take care of her family. As I ponder this realization, the moral of her story dawns on me, and the takeaway becomes clear. While the narrative surrounding substance use disor-der may appear to be simple on the surface, the human complexity underneath it is always daunting.

Jeanne understands certain things about her past better now, like why her dad always carried a weapon. But there are some things she won't talk about at all—not for this book and not even in conversa-tion with me off the record. The wounds are too fresh, and the dark-ness overwhelms her. She tries to maintain a healthy practice of self-reflection, but this is difficult. She's not always sure what to bring up and what to leave behind, especially when it comes to her kids, whom she doesn't want to burden with unnecessary disclosures about things that happened before their time.

Her husband, whose own son died of a drug overdose not long ago, says that some things are better left in the past. I can understand this feeling, as I'm sure many people do. To emphasize this point, Jeanne recalls the time she told her story in a small group and it "wrecked her for three days." That was the first time she looked back and realized how bad and depressing her life had been before she got sober.

Our conversation is ending now, almost out of necessity. "Do you think you're still carrying unresolved trauma?" I ask. She says nothing, but her eyes begin to fill with tears, so I leave it alone. For Jeanne, what matters right now is this: "My family doesn't need to live in that chaos." Silence hangs in the air between us. The words of Dr. Gabor Maté return to me: *"Don't ask 'why the addiction,' but 'why the pain.'"*

"I FEEL LIKE I'VE GAINED MY OWN SELF BACK."

They say that addiction is a family affair. Not only does the person suffering with substance use disorder go through hell, but the people around them do, too. Each one is affected in their own way.

The concept of *co-dependency* arose early in the history of Alcoholics Anonymous in reference to the person who is in a dysfunctional relationship with an abuser. The New Oxford Dictionary defines the condition as being marked by "excessive emotional or psychological reliance on a partner, typically one who requires support on account of an illness or addiction." In short, the co-dependent is a person who becomes enmeshed in their loved one's destructive patterns to the point of harm. This happens all the time in cases of drug addiction.

Alicia's story highlights the struggle of co-dependency. I did my best to capture that struggle in her own words, but the raw intensity in her voice spoke more deeply to the subject than these pages will successfully relate. Although some of her scars are still relatively fresh, it appeared to me that she is doing what it takes to work through her pain. She's finding ways to integrate all the elements of her past, even those that hurt, into a new story she is now writing for herself and her kids.

⊖ ⊖ ⊖

"Like most folks, my childhood was less than ideal," Alicia begins. "My parents divorced when I was two years old and my stepdad was abusive. At some point he crossed the line. I was fourteen when I met my ex-husband. Our relationship was volatile almost from the start; there was a lot of emotional abuse. Over time, it eroded my self-confidence."

Alicia's relationship with her ex went back and forth for many years. "I joined the military in July 2003," she says. "After returning home, we got back together … again. I became pregnant in June the following year. I kept thinking things would be ok." She shakes her head in disbelief. "We finally got married in 2009. That was four months after he shattered my finger."

A second child arrived, then a third, and then a fourth. Her ex was in and out of treatment during those years. "His mom is really the one who held the marriage together," Alicia recalls. "She and I were very close. She was the glue."

Despite the continuing abuse, that glue held out for eight long years. During the summer of 2017, Alicia finally began to see the damage that was being done to her kids. Alarm bells went off inside her head and she began praying for the strength to leave.

"It happened on my thirty-third birthday that year," she says. "That's when I finally said *enough* and gathered the strength to take my kids and run. It took several attempts and involved the help of many friends and even the law, but I did it. I went into hiding for a while before moving in with my mother in Kentucky. At first, he would show up at my work here and there and try to call. One time he even followed me from work—from Otway all the way to the Greenup dam. I literally ran a red light, swooped in and swerved around the gas station to lose him. But at that point, I think he started to realize he was fighting a losing battle and that I wasn't coming back. It's still been kind of touch-and-go since then. He doesn't see the kids all that much. He's been in and out of treatment several times."

Alicia got a protection order from the court and spent a lot of time hiding out. Through teary eyes, she describes the whole ordeal as a "nightmare." The divorce was finalized in January 2018, and although the kids still see their dad on occasion, not all of them want to.

"I let him see the two younger ones on Father's Day in 2018. The two older ones didn't want to go. That's the day he left his brother's house (where they were staying) and went to another brother's house, where he ended up overdosing with the kids in the car."

With the kids in the car. I sit back in my chair and absorb the impact of that statement. That was the last time any of Alicia's kids had seen their dad until recently. At the time of our interview, he had been back in treatment and was starting to receive supervised calls and visits again.

"What comes to your mind when you think of him now?" I ask.

Alicia answers almost without thought, "Disgust," she says. "I mean, really—yeah. I feel like, if it wasn't for my kids ... I know in my heart of hearts that my kids are the only thing good that came out of the two of us." She laughs nervously. "Because when I look back and consider all the missed opportunities and how much I let go—I mean, I was a good student! I was at the top of my class at vo-tech. I had actually started college at one point, but he didn't like that. He would rip up essays I was working on because he didn't want to wait for me to go through college like he waited on me through high school.

"I threw away my military career, too. The sign-on bonus, free college ... I lost it all because of him. So, when I look back at all the opportunities I lost and everything I put on hold, when I think of him, I feel only disgust. Disgust and regret. I also feel disappointed with myself. I'm disappointed that I allowed someone to have so much power over me and to take away my sense of self-worth like he did."

Of course, this kind of admission always comes with a caveat. "How have you changed since then?" I ask.

Alicia looks beyond me and smiles. "The irony of the whole situation is that if I hadn't been through all that, I wouldn't be where I am today," she answers. "What I hold onto is the belief that I went through all of this, so I can be a light to somebody else. That I can help someone who's been in my shoes, who feels like there is no hope or that they are all alone.

"I mean, I've worked very hard to educate myself on addiction. I don't wish ill on my ex-husband. Since he got out of treatment this last time, I've heard that he is using again, but I don't want to see anyone lost to addiction, not even him. Even with everything he put me through, and even though I don't feel able to reach out a hand to him myself, he's still a soul."

These are more than just words. I've seen firsthand Alicia's passion not just for her children but for the community. She's devoted one hundred percent to helping other people find their way. "Over the past few years, I feel like I've gained a lot of my own strength and own self back," she says. "That's the journey I'm on now. I'm pushing through to make a better future for myself and my kids."

Of course, recovering from co-dependency is easier said than done. Crippling feelings of self-doubt still rear their ugly head from time to time, especially when Alicia thinks about her children.

"People tell me all the time that they notice the difference in me," she says. "That they see a light in my eyes that wasn't there before. And my kids are happier than they've ever been. But it helps to hear that from other people. When you separate your kids from everything they've known—even though it was toxic—you start to doubt yourself. You ask yourself, *Am I doing the right thing? Am I destroying their future?*

"More than anything else, though, I pray that my daughters know they don't have to accept and be with the type of person I was with. And I pray that my son never treats a woman that way. Of course, I also pray that none of them ever let addiction get ahold of them in any way whatsoever."

Alicia's kids are still relatively young, but she thinks they have a decent grasp on the situation. Her ten-year old struggles the most because she's the closest to her dad and shares the same co-dependent traits that Alicia had with her ex. The older kids miss their dad but are glad to be free from the life they were living before. They have both expressed this feeling to Alicia in no uncertain terms, even assuring her that if she ever goes back to their dad, no matter how much he seems to have changed, they *won't* be sticking around.

"About a year after the divorce," Alicia says, "my oldest son came to me and said, 'You don't know how much I prayed for this. Every time Dad hurt you, he hurt me. I prayed that you would leave and stay gone forever.' Those are incredible words coming from a thirteen-year old.

"But yeah, for a while after I first left, I wondered what I was think-ing." She laughs. "I thought to myself, 'Now I'm never going to have this or that.' That's what I was brainwashed into thinking all those years, after all. That I could never make it on my own and that I would never be worth anything to someone else. But here I am. I've made it and I've accomplished so much. I will only continue to grow!"

These days, Alicia stays busy working with her friends and family at RAW Addiction. What initially drew her to the group was the dra-matic change she witnessed in its founder, John Evans.

"My story is a good example of how RAW Addiction helps people," Alicia says. "They stepped in to help me. Like they say, recovery from drug addiction looks different for different people. Well, recovering from being co-dependent with someone in addiction looks different for different people, too. When you're stuck in that place, you become a person you don't even know yourself. But being around positive people helped me change my way of thinking. They helped me realize that it's ok to think about me and what I need, too."

"To see what John was trying to do in the community, and the example he was setting—I thought, *Wow, this is big.*" Alicia followed John's work online, and the two of them eventually became friends. "Shortly after that, John reached out to me about starting another group for the loved ones of people in addiction. I was thrilled. Having him ask me to lead this group was the biggest honor I've ever received, so, of course, I graciously accepted."

Other women with similar experiences began to come on board, and in April 2018, RAW Addiction: Through the Eyes of Loved Ones was born.

"We're kind of the backbone of RAW Addiction," Alicia says, laughing. "Really, though, we're a big family. We're working together to bring change not only to our community but to communities around the world, to bring light in a world that is full of so much darkness. We want to bring people together rather than tear each other apart. Change and togetherness is what we need to end this epidemic—it's simply a must! We are all here together as a family, a RAW family, sharing the same passion to help people in need! Our passion is what I think sets us apart."

Alicia and her friends at RAW put their money where their mouth is, too. All the community events they host, including coat drives, soup kitchens, and Christmas plays, have been funded either by local donations or out of their own pockets. The kids always seem to have a blast at these events as well. In fact, seeing the impact on her children is probably what impresses Alicia the most.

"We focus a lot on trying to get the kids involved, letting them know that there are other things besides drugs and that they don't always have to be in that chaos, that they can have fun without all of that. Now they will pick up on other kids at school who seem to be going through the things they've gone through. They'll come home and say, 'Mom, there's this student, and I can tell they are going through things at home. I really want to help them.' The next generation is already facing down the drug crisis in their own way.

"That's what it's all about. For myself, I'm continuing my education. I'm working hard to show my kids that not everything is handed to you in life. My long-term goal is to see the loved ones group launch nationwide. This will always be my top priority. I have big plans and ideas for RAW Addiction—I know we all do—and I don't doubt for a moment that it's going to happen. That's what I want to do, to be engaged full-time in this kind of work."

I'm impressed by Alicia's drive. Her personality reminds me of a gentle river on a peaceful day, all quiet on the surface but raging with deep intensity in the currents down below. Since our interview, she has given birth to another beautiful baby girl and is preparing to enter the Police Academy to pursue a career in law enforcement. Although the wreckage of addiction is not that far behind her, she is moving on now and making peace with her past.

"It's like how an addict has to hit their rock bottom," she explains. "Loved ones have to hit their rock bottom, too, and just hope that it's not a casket. For me, I had to grow a backbone and convince myself that I didn't need my ex-husband, that I was worse off with him than without him, and that I *could* rebuild."

Alicia emphasizes that word "could" as if she finally believes it. Listening to her, knowing how much history and heartache lies behind it, I can't help but believe it too.

"I HAD TO RE-EVALUATE HOW I THOUGHT ABOUT PEOPLE WITH DRUG ADDICTION."

E dwin didn't grow up in southern Ohio. He landed in the city of Portsmouth after a long road of family trauma took him from Cleveland to Florida and back again in search of a home. Now he works at The Counseling Center, southern Ohio's largest treatment provider with forty locations across three counties, where he teaches automotive skills to people in recovery. He also serves as Portsmouth's first ever Hispanic councilmember.

Edwin and I sat down together for about an hour one evening after he got off work. His story could easily demonstrate the complexity of drug addiction from any number of angles, but what stood out to me was the way Edwin began to empathize with the needs of people who use drugs after learning about the trauma behind his own mother's substance use disorder. Despite the pain that Edwin still carries over the way he was mistreated as a child, he's found a way to move beyond his individual perspective to become an ally to folks in recovery.

All I can say is, may his tribe increase.

⊖ ⊖ ⊖

"I was born and raised in Lorain, OH," Edwin begins. "Like many small towns across the state, it was once a nice city. Big and booming, it had a steel plant and a Ford manufacturing plant. But they left and then everything pretty much went to ruin. That was back in the 80's. They're still struggling to make things work. It reminds me a lot of Portsmouth in that sense.

"My family has always been, uh ... 'hardened criminals' would probably be the best way to describe it." He chuckles. "My grandmother was definitely a con artist. She pretty much stole me away from my father when I was about eight years old using the court system. She was able to do that because, as you know, we have a broken system. She took me as far away as she could, which was Florida. She was a drug user. She would smoke pot, snort coke, pop pills ... she was also a manipulator. She knew how to con the system. It's fascinating in a way, but also not—you know what I mean? It's like, 'Wow, how are you able to do that?'

"There were times I would go with her to pick up a baggie or something from a dealer. Mind you, I'm ten or eleven years old at that point. We'd find a parking lot and she would say to me, 'Alright, I need you to look out.' So, I would look out and she would sit there and bump a line real quick. Being around that stuff over the years made me feel a certain way. Just watching the destruction was hard. Drugs would lead to violence and then to incarceration. Always living off the system. Never being able to really have fun or go anywhere—take trips or vacations—nothing like that.

"My grandmother was one thing, but my mother was on a totally different level. My grandmother had custody of me, but it was always hit or miss with my mom when she was around. She was either on drugs—heroin was her drug of choice—or she was fighting to get her children back. She would try to do things the right way, but then something would happen and she'd just be gone again. Having to see her incarcerated all the time was hard.

"I remember this one time when I was young. She picked me up from my grandma's and I was gonna spend the weekend with her. She had a little apartment and stuff. And for some reason—I don't know what her thinking was—she had me in the room with her while she was getting ready to shoot up. She had the spoon and aluminum foil out, the rubber band ... I was young enough to not really know what she was doing, but old enough to know that it didn't seem right. She told me to turn around and not watch. 'Don't look at me,' she said. But all I can remember is turning around and standing in front of a mirror and being able to see every aspect of what she was doing."

Edwin pauses. His eyes grow red. He sits back in his chair and stretches a hand up to touch his ponytail. He looks uncomfortable. I can tell he is re-living the moment, probably for the thousandth time.

"You know, I'm thirty-seven years old now," he says. "I've seen a lot of things, but for some reason, that image is forever ingrained in my brain."

He stops again before continuing.

"I got to the point where I always knew when she was using," he says. "It was so constant that I could recognize the signs. I didn't even have to look at her; I could hear it in her voice. But you know, I got to where I saw all of this destruction and damage. All of the relationships that were destroyed. My heart has been broken by my mother so many times, man. It's frustrating. There are seven of us kids in the family. All of us have different fathers and I'm the oldest. None of us were raised by our mother, but it got to the point where all that I could think about were my brothers and sisters, trying to figure out, 'How do I keep them away from this? How do I set an example that doesn't involve destroying their lives?' So, eventually I had to make a choice, and it was tough.

"When I was sixteen or seventeen years old, I was trying really hard to get my education and be able to play sports, basketball especially. But no matter what I did, I was always falling short of my goals because something was going on at home that was affecting me. I was so angry with people all the time because of it. I didn't understand this then, but I understand it now. I was expelled from schools for fighting. I didn't even care if I got my butt whooped. If someone looked at me wrong, that was enough. I was looking for a fight. I was dealing with so much anger from my family that I look back now and think it's a miracle that I am where I am today. I could have easily fallen into the system and never found my way out.

"But just to give you an example of what my grandmother is like, and what she did to my mother, consider this: There were points where my mom would get her life together and start doing things right. She'd get a job and an apartment. At one point she was even taking classes. She would fight and make it work and get her kids back from the court. Everything was cool. But then my grandma would start feeling the loss of that extra check, right? One time when that happened, she called Child Protective Services anonymously and told them that my brothers were living with a convicted felon and that the situation was really bad for them at home. So, they took the kids and put them back with my grandma."

Edwin shakes his head in disbelief. "It's no wonder my mom had all kinds of issues," he says. "Later in life, I asked her, 'Why?' and she told me a story about being in Puerto Rico with my grandmother. There were parties going on all the time at their house. Guys would come and take advantage of my mom and my grandma would do nothing about it. My mom was being abused by random dudes when she was twelve years old, man. It's no wonder she has stuff that she's dealing with. I didn't know any of that growing up. All this time I was holding resentment against my mother for her behavior and I had no idea what was behind it all. I grew up thinking that my mom did drugs just because she wanted to and nothing else.

"This belief led to me feeling resentment in general, not just toward her but toward anyone who lived that kind of lifestyle. So, I grew up with the notion that people who are addicted to drugs simply *choose* to forget about their loved ones and put that needle in their arm. They *choose* to hurt their children. It wasn't until just a few years ago that I began to realize my mom's drug use was more than a simple choice ... that it was about her trying to deal with stuff she didn't know how to deal with.

"In that sense, it's crazy that my life has brought me to Portsmouth, where I'm smack dab in the middle of this opioid epidemic and offering my help to people who I always thought were the bad ones. I talk to people now whose stories are amazing. Hurtful, sad, and crazy, yes, but amazing. And through it all, I keep thinking about my mom. After thirty-seven years, I'm still trying to have a relationship with my mother. She's not getting any younger. I'm not getting any younger. Yet here we are, still struggling to have some kind of mother-son relationship. At this point, I don't even know if it will ever happen, the mother-son thing. Maybe we could be acquaintances?"

Edwin shakes his head at his own question, which is obviously not rhetorical. He's genuinely trying to work this out.

"I don't know," he finally admits. "I've gotten to the point where I had to remove the negativity from my life. I don't want my children to experience anything near what I had to go through. That's why I made the decision I did when I was sixteen. I had to get out. I was starting to get into it, and I had to get out. I told myself, 'No, I do not want my life to be like theirs. I want something more. So, I picked up my stuff and left. I got a job at AutoZone. I had to drop out of school to go to work, but I used my first paycheck to buy a '92 Mitsubishi Mirage. I lived in my car in the parking lot because I had nowhere else to go. It was a choice I had to make to survive, though. That's what it was about for me."

"Where was your dad in all of this?" I ask.

"Dad was about a thousand miles away, back in Ohio," Edwin says. "You know, he tried. He really did try. He would try to have a relationship with me but I always pushed him away. Maybe 'pushed him away' isn't the best way to describe it. It's just hard when you're young to have a relationship with someone over the phone. So, he tried, but I just wasn't going to have a relationship over the phone. I didn't want to tell him certain things about what I was dealing with because I knew he felt responsible."

"Do you think he's responsible?" I ask.

"No," he replies quickly. "Dad fought. He really did try. He fought my whole life, man. It wasn't until I went through my divorce that I finally opened up to him, and when I needed him, he was there for me."

Edwin leans forward in his chair. His eyes grow red again and his voice cracks.

"It's crazy, because I fought really hard to build something. When I moved out and I was living in my car, my ex-wife's parents ended up taking me in. Her father was one of those hard-ass types, you know what I mean? He didn't play games. He was a man's man. I had a lot of respect for him because of that. He talked to me like I needed to be talked to, like a man. He sat me down and said, 'Listen, if you're going to be here in my house, you won't have to worry about anything. You'll have all the food and shelter you need. The only thing that I ask of you is that you do something with yourself. The first thing I want you to do is go back to school and get your diploma.' I said, 'Ok,' and I did. After that, he said, 'Now what are you gonna do?' I didn't know what to do at that point, so he offered to pay for me to go to trade school. I did some research and decided to become a mechanic. He paid for a year of school, and after that I got a job changing oil at a Firestone. Life started to get better from there. My girlfriend and I married and we got an apartment. We had a son. Everything was going great. Fantastic. I felt like I had actually built something.

"But then it all came crashing down," he says, snapping his fingers, "just like that. I'd known my ex-wife for a long time. We were high school sweethearts. Best friends. We had a lot of history. It was up and down, but for the most part, we loved each other. We grew apart, though, and it came crashing down. We both started seeking love in other people; that wasn't healthy. So, we called it quits. I thought we were in agreement about things, but it got ugly. It got to the point where I was back to living in my car. She got everything else. I even lost my job. This affected me to the point where I didn't even know who I was anymore. And then, out of nowhere, my mom came back into the picture. She told me she was doing well and asked me to come stay with her, and I did."

Edwin takes a deep breath.

"You know, there were moments in life where mom was a mom," he says, "and those brief moments were everything that I lived for. Those were the moments I had wanted all my life. And in that moment, mom was my savior. But then it happened. All the sudden, she was smoking weed and drinking again. The next thing you know, I hear a tow truck outside one night repossessing my car. Everything I owned was inside it." He shakes his head. "There were also situations involving mom's man being drunk and me having to forcefully remove him from the house. It made me remember why I left in the first place, so I got out again.

"I couldn't find a job anywhere at the time, though. I thought about going into the military, but that didn't work out either. My dad was sending me money here and there just so I could eat, but finally he said, 'I'm not sending you anymore money, I'm sending a plane ticket. One way.' So, I moved back to the Cleveland area and stayed in my dad's basement. This was around 2011. I went out and got two jobs on the first day. Like I said, my dad was there for me when I needed him. We began to build a relationship. Things were good, but I started to get really depressed being away from my son. It was devastating for me to have to leave him behind. I would cry myself to sleep every night."

Edwin's pace slows down at this point. He begins to measure his words. I can tell he is approaching an important point in the story.

"One day, dad sat me down," he says. "He put his arm around me and said, 'I know how you feel.'"

Edwin leans forward and claps his hands together lightly. "I was just like, 'Wow.' You know what I mean? God. That pain … " He wipes his eye. "It was so hard, man. Don't get me wrong, it still is. But I've been able to manage and cope better since then. It's crazy how my life has come full circle with my dad. He experienced the same thing with me that I'm experiencing now with my son. Being separated and having to talk on the phone, feeling like we don't really have a relationship … for him to say, 'I understand how you feel' was so real. He said, 'But one day, your son is gonna need you and you've just got to be ready to be there.'

"The more I keep thinking about it, like—I just don't, you know … " Edwin stumbles over his words, apparently at a loss. "It's just that I've never … " He pauses again and finally lands on something solid.

"If there's one thing my family taught me, it was what *not* to do. So, I always told myself to not be like them. 'Don't do it, because it will lead you places you don't want to go'—that's what I told myself. I mean, I *wanted* to smoke weed. I wanted to drink. But seeing the destruction it brought to everyone in my family just broke my heart, so I would think to myself, "I can't do that. Don't do it.' No matter how depressed I got, I never used drugs as a way to cope.

"And that brings me back to my changing view on drug addicts. Remember, everything in my life early on made me believe that drug addiction was just a choice, right? Because I went through some really stupid stuff. I was molested when I was a kid, just four years old. I was living at my grandma's house and the babysitter abused me. Dealing with drugs in the house all the time. Being poor even though my grandmother had plenty of money from welfare, social security, and child support from my dad. Being depressed, having to deal with losing my son through my divorce, plus the fact that I don't have a relationship with my mother, which has affected me in ways I can't even understand. Yet, I made the choice to not use drugs in response to all of that. And it was freaking hard, man. There were times in my life when things were just passing me by. Other kids were getting to experience life, go on trips, play sports, and have a supportive family … but who was there at my basketball games? No one. Who dropped me off and picked me up from practice? No one. Who helped me with my homework? No one."

Edwin looks at the wall in front of him and shakes his head.

"I had to rely on people who weren't even part of my family. You know, here's this couple with a daughter who I happened to be dating, who have more love for someone that they don't even know … "

He starts choking up at this thought. I look down at the floor, hardly able to contain my own tears. The way Edwin talks about having no one to bring him to basketball practice or come to his games reminds me of my own dad, now gone, who wouldn't have missed one of my games for the world. It just isn't fair that Edwin didn't get to experience that kind of support at no fault of his own.

"Not once did I give in to the temptation to use drugs as a way to cope, though," he says. "I don't know what made me that kind of anomaly. Whatever it was, it led me to think that other people who did have an addiction were there just because of their own choices and nothing more. But I was so wrong to think that."

Edwin composes himself, then continues.

"To finish the story, though, I came back to Ohio, where I found a job. Actually, I worked two jobs for a little bit. I started to get my stuff together. Next thing you know, I got a car and moved out of my dad's house. That's when I met my current wife. Things progressed really fast with her. She was a single mom and she had two kids of her own, just trying to make things work. We got ahold of each other and decided that we wanted to spend our lives together.

"We used to come to southern Ohio to see my brother-in-law. He would always invite us to come for visits. And I just loved it down here. Portsmouth was definitely good to me. I was like, 'Man, people are so nice.' I mean, people who didn't even know me would wave at me!" He laughs. "You know what I mean? They hold doors open for you. I swear sometimes I live in Pleasantville. When we first moved here, a neighbor even brought us dinner! Who does that? So, I loved it. It was like coming home. And then ... Then, I found out that my mom had cancer."

Edwin leans forward in his chair and places his head in his hands. When he looks up again, his eyes are filled with tears.

"After I wrote her off for years," he says. "I mean, I tried my hardest to do something with her. But it always, always ended up hurting me.

And then I got this news, and it hit me so hard. I couldn't function. I couldn't do anything. All I could think about was *not having that chance*. That's what kept running through my mind—the thought that now, if something happened to her, I wasn't going to have that opportunity to make things right and have a relationship with my mom.

"So, the cancer brought us together again. I supported her. Anything she needed, I was there. I flew the whole family out to see her. I tried to spend as much time as I could with her. Anything I could do, I tried. Then one day, she called and said, 'I need your help. I need a place to stay.' Something in me just blurted out, 'Yes, for sure. You can come here.'"

A somber expression spreads across Edwin's face. "That decision almost destroyed my relationship with my wife," he says, "for a couple reasons. One, she knows a little about my story and things that have happened in the past. Two, she doesn't really know my mom. And three, that wasn't just my decision to make. But I made the assumption that it would be ok because, you know, it was my mom. That turned into a really trying time, though. I would say it's the most trying time my wife and I have ever gone through.

"Mom moved here and stayed with us for a while. Eventually, she got her own place. She was seeing a cancer doctor here and things were going good. She loved the area. My relationship with my wife got rocky but seemed to improve after a while. Then one day my step-daughter ran away from home. She and my mom had been developing a relationship which was more of a friendship than a grandmother-granddaughter thing. I allowed it to happen because I thought things were going to be different this time, you know? But I'm like that battered woman who's always sticking up for the person beating on her. That's what life was like for me with my mom. She would come into my life and beat me up a little bit, then I would say, 'I can't do this anymore' and leave, but then later on we'd get together and do it all over again. It was a cycle.

"But I thought for sure this time was going to be different. Mom had cancer. She was living in a place where people were genuinely nice to her. It was the kind of environment you'd think would propel her to be a better mom. But nope. Making that assumption was a huge mistake on my part.

"So, my daughter ran away one evening. We had friends and family out looking for her. We had cops knocking on doors, searching houses for her. Just all over the place. And my mom is calling me, asking, 'Oh, have you found her yet? I'm so concerned.' But then my daughter made the mistake of texting a friend of hers, saying, 'Hey, I'm at my grandma's house hiding in the basement.' Well, this girl told her parents and her parents told us. I thought to myself, 'There's no way.' I mean, my wife was literally at my mom's house, sitting and crying to my mom about her daughter, and my mom was like, 'Oh my gosh, I don't know what I'd do if I were you.' And the whole time, my daughter was in the next room.

"I went to my mom's house and while I was still outside, I called her and said, 'Hey, are you sure my daughter's not with you?' She began to act upset that I didn't believe her. I said, 'Ok, well, I'll be there in just a few minutes, and if you don't mind, I want to look through the house.' Little did she know that I was already sitting outside. We hung up the phone, and boom, she shuts off all the lights in the house and my daughter comes walking out the back door. I just about lost my mind."

A deep breath.

"That's the last time I spoke to my mother," he says. "It's been about three years. I wrestled with guilt over it. I thought, 'How can I can kick her to the curb again when she's got cancer and she's dealing with all this stuff? But I had to protect my family. I don't want my daughter growing up thinking this is how people treat each other and that it's ok. I had to call it quits again, and this time for real.

"My relationship with my mother is never gonna happen," he says, shaking his head. "One of us will die, and that will be it. My mother matters to me, but I'm going to have to live with that, knowing that it's just never going to happen."

Something about Edwin's posture and tone of voice makes this sound like a moment of truth for him. I nod my head, acknowledging the gravity of his situation. As much as I hate to admit it, the best thing that can happen to some relationships is for them to simply end.

"Since then, my relationship with my daughter has improved," he says. "She has her own issues with her biological father, who was never around. She pushed me away some because she couldn't understand why I would be around when he wasn't. But since she's gotten a little older, we have a great relationship. I have a beautiful family, man. Things have been looking up for me.

"But like I told you, I always had this notion of drug addiction as nothing more than a bad choice. The reason I thought that was because of the things I saw in my life growing up. I saw how easy it would have been for me to use drugs to cope with my pain, but I chose something different for myself. That's me, though. What about people who aren't strong enough to do that? Am I supposed to resent these kids who were literally born addicted? Should I tell them it was their choice? That doesn't make any sense.

"So, I had to re-evaluate who I was and how I thought about people with drug addiction. I've found that being a part of our youth here in the city of Portsmouth—maybe I could use my story to help some of these kids who are going through things similar to what I went through. And some of these kids have it harder than I did, man. So, whatever I can do to help around the community, I'm there. I play ball with the kids. I'm a mentor in our juvenile drug court. The more I got involved, the more I saw how I could make a difference.

"Along with that, I started doing research to learn what drug addiction really is. Why do people even use drugs? Most of the time, it's due to trauma of some sort. Understanding this is what led me to work at The Counseling Center, where I teach automotive skills to people with drug addiction. I give them skills that no one will be able to take away from them, skills they can use to better their lives. You know, we talk a lot about rehab and it's usually just drug use that we have in mind, but rehab is about a whole lot more than just drugs. 95% of the people I work with need their entire life rehabbed, not just the part where they use drugs.

"Of course, it's true that there are some people who just started using for whatever reason and now they have a hard time getting off it. But for most people, they are dealing with something intense and that's what led to the drug use. Combine that with the overwhelming number of babies who are born with addiction these days, and how can I be mad at people about that? How can I resent them for it? How can I justify telling people that drug addiction is just a choice? The best thing I can do is provide a healthy environment for my kids so that they never feel the need to go down that path. This is what I've made it my mission to do. I work really, really hard to make sure they have everything they need. And I'm going do everything I can to help other people along the way."

"IF I CONTINUE DOWN THIS PATH, IT'S JUST A MATTER OF TIME."

Public health workers estimate that one out of five people in the United States have some sort of diagnosable mental illness. This figure amounts to about *60 million people*, many of whom feel very much alone in their experience. At the same time, there are only about 500,000 qualified mental health practitioners out there, most of whom are over the age of sixty and nearing retirement.[9] Young people don't want to go into a field that promises a mountain of student loan debt with uncertain income returns due to the hesitation of insurance providers to recognize and cover psychological issues.

These ratios suggest not only a current mental health crisis of epic proportions, but a looming catastrophe that is going to be far worse than the present devastation if our policies and practices don't catch up soon. God only knows how many people are living and dying somewhere beneath the cracks. People like Chris Howard.

Throughout the process of interviewing people for this book, I looked for someone who was still actively using drugs to tell me about their experience. I wanted to speak with someone who was still caught in the thick of it, whose perspective was informed not just by looking back but by looking within and around them in the present moment.

---

9   In the words of clinical psychologist Randy Phelps, who shared these statistics during a 320 Festival panel discussion, "That's one hell of a case load!"

With Chris, I got all that and more. In fact, I probably enjoyed my conversation with Chris more than any other for how it illuminated the lessons I've been learning about addiction over the past few years. I can't say that I'm happy about these observations, because after all, most of them weren't very encouraging. Nevertheless, Chris helped me see further into the dynamic interplay of poverty, domestic violence, mental illness, and incarceration among people who suffer with substance use disorder. For a few fragile moments, he pulled back the curtain over his life and allowed me to view the world from where he stands. I'll always be grateful for this courageous act of vulnerability.

$$\ominus \quad \ominus \quad \ominus$$

"I should start by saying that this is an on-going struggle for me," Chris says, sitting down in a chair by the door in my office. "Yesterday was yesterday. Today, I haven't had anything yet, and hopefully that's how I'll end the day, but it's a battle."

Chris's eyes dart back and forth between the floor and the desk between us. I notice they are already turning red.

"Sorry," he says, shaking his head. "I'm trying to keep my composure." He reaches for the box of tissues on the desk, pauses to wipe his eyes, then apologizes again.

"I get a little upset because … " He glances down the hall where his friend, John Evans, who brought him to this meeting, is sitting. "I have to steer clear of John usually because he's a reminder of where I should be. It's hard being around him. Talking about any of this is hard for me in general. I'm currently struggling, you know. Trying to find my place in the world. I don't think that place exists, though."

I can tell Chris is having a hard time getting into his story. Hoping to jumpstart the process, I ask, "Did you grow up around here?"

"Oh yeah, I'm a West-Sider," he says. "My mom still lives up that way. Officially, I live in the ville[10], but I stay with her a lot." He pauses. "Look, I'm just gonna give you the uncut version here and hope that anything I say doesn't come back to bite me. I'm pretty much beat into submission at this point, anyway."

I nod. "Fair enough."

"So, I guess you've probably heard the familiar story of how people talk about their upbringing," Chris continues. "Obviously, that does have a huge impact on what happens with a person as they grow older. For me, it's a safe bet to say that I was never gonna be anything other than a criminal. That is, if you consider my upbringing. Of course, that can also be an easy scapegoat for people's problems. I'm a grown man, and I made my own decisions. I know right from wrong. While my childhood was pretty devastating, I guess it could have made me stronger.

"I've spent more time in confinement than I have in the free world, and I'm forty-nine years old. I've been sentenced by a court on thirteen separate occasions. And even though I'm struggling right now, every morning I wake up not in jail I'm setting a new record. This is the longest I've ever been out, about ten months since February. That's really nothing to boast about, but I'm in uncharted territory nonetheless."

"How does that make you feel?" I ask.

"To me, it's not even an accomplishment," Chris responds. "Because I feel like if I continue down this path, it's just a matter of time. At the same time, I can say that a few things have changed. I don't steal anymore. I work. I just don't think ... It's just that the picture I painted

---

10 A local slang expression for the low-income housing project on the north side of town.

as a juvenile—I don't like that guy. He was a terrible guy, and that's why people are scared of me today. I don't like that."

"Are you still connected with your family?" I ask.

"Oh, yeah. I just saw my mom before I came here. The adult parole authority thinks I live with my sister, but really, I live with my mom," he says. "The truth of the matter is, if I had gone to my sister's, I'd probably already be back in jail. Not from robbing somebody or anything like that, but when you live this kind of lifestyle, crazy things just happen. It's part of the package. Like I said, though, I don't blame anyone other than myself. Yeah, my step-dad was a monster and all that, but he doesn't make my decisions for me now."

Chris moves around in his chair as if he's looking for just the right spot.

"Well, I might as well just start back at the top, huh? My mom met my step-dad in '72 or '73. I was two or three years old at the time. Mom was still with my father, then, and he was a pretty terrible individual. I don't have a lot of recollection because I was so young, but he beat on my mom. The only real memory I have from that time—and it's so long ago that I don't know if I'm remembering the incident or just remembering, remembering it—was how he broke us kids from sucking our thumbs by putting hot sauce on them. But, yeah, he beat on my mom every single day it seemed like. She has mental health issues now which is probably a result of the abuse. She doesn't use drugs, though. She's pretty amazing.

"But, yeah, he was a terrible man. We lived in Tampa, FL for a while, and I used to come in every day and listen to my dad beat up my mom. I guess he just got tired of it, and one day he asked her if she wanted to leave. She said yeah, and we hurried up and left. Which was a good idea because he probably would have changed his mind pretty quickly. Mom claims that he was a killer for the mafia.

"So, we came back around 1975. We moved to Columbus for a few years then returned to West Portsmouth. My step-dad bought a trailer and built onto it and turned it into a house. We had a little bit of normalcy in our lives at that point. In 1981, though, Mom got a job at the derby and started fooling around with one of her co-workers. My step-dad had also done the same thing with her sister first. Obviously, two wrongs don't make a right, but that's what began my criminal career. They tried to work it out a few times, but they split up.

"Man, some of the fights I seen, though. He would never punch her, I'll give him credit for that, but man—my mom would get irate. Like, one day he was trying to hold on to her outside while all us kids were in the house, and the next thing you know I see this axe just come flying through the door. It barely missed his head.

"Finally, they split up. Mom filed for custody, but all of us kids wanted to stay with him because we could get away with more stuff. Eventually, I just started getting in trouble because he didn't care what we did. Then when the law got involved on multiple occasions, he tried to reel me in. Roofing and construction was his thing, and he tried to get me into that, but I don't know—at that point I was lost. I was just a crazy kid. I started smoking weed and drinking at a very young age, like around eight years old. I was twelve the first time I got in trouble with the law. That's when I spent some time in a group home in South Webster.

"My criminal career just blossomed from there. I stole everything that wasn't nailed down. I mean, we could drive around this town, and I'd have a hard time showing you all the places I've broken into. I don't want that to sound like I'm bragging because I don't like that guy. I'm ashamed, you know. I've terrorized this town. Everywhere I go, I leave a stain."

Chris shifts uncomfortably in his chair again.

"I don't know," he continues. "Child psychologists believe that, you know, most of our subconscious is developed during the ages of 3-5. That's a hard pill to swallow, to say that the main ingredients of your character are already developed at that point." He looks at the floor and shakes his head. "I don't know. Everybody tried to give me other chances. My parents wanted to just leave me in the county, but as a juvenile you have a little more flexibility when it comes to being in jail. The only time you're gonna stay in jail is if the judge orders you to. Otherwise, your family can come and get you. Excluding the group home, I went to jail for the first time in 1985. Since then, I've spent less than one year at a time in the free world."

"Have you been to treatment?" I ask.

"Oh yeah," Chris responds. "I could teach a class myself right now. Cognitive Behavioral Therapy (CBT). I could literally teach a class. I'm not saying that to brag, just to point out how ineffective it is. I know it's the big thing now. Everybody loves CBT. But they're missing one major ingredient, in my opinion. This is what I struggle with. People have to have the pieces in their lives that make them want to *not* do drugs and commit crimes. They need to have stakes in their life. If they don't have them …

"Well, take CBT, for instance. The premise is that if you stop and think about the decision before you make it, you can challenge it. And that's all good and fine. But if I don't have the pieces in my life that I need, it doesn't matter. I'll make that bad decision regardless. It's made for me already in my subconscious."

"What do you mean by having the right 'pieces'?" I ask.

"People you care about, like a girlfriend or a wife," Chris says. "A career, or something you're passionate about. Identity is something that a lot of people struggle with, you know. They say that a person with no identity suffers a fate worse than death. That's how I feel. I've tried to grab onto certain things throughout the years, but … I don't know."

He glances down the hallway.

"John is probably doing the kind of thing more than anyone I know that would help me stay clean," he says, pausing for a long minute to hold back his tears. "John's living it. I gotta be honest, he's defied the odds. I mean, people listen to all this stuff in prison, right? Me and him were in the Horizon program together. The difference is, he came out and put it into practice. He's got room to grow just like everybody does, and he's got lessons to learn about how much he can really help people, but, you know … I don't want it to seem like I'm taking a shot at him, but nobody can provide someone else the resources that they need. They just can't. The biggest decision has to be made from within. It's something that can't be given to you. Or maybe only God can give it to you.

"This big treatment phase we're in right now is gonna be short-lived, though. At least, I believe it is. Only eleven percent of the population gets better. Those are not numbers our politicians are gonna continue to throw money at. They're just not. So, I give this treatment phase maybe ten more years. I'm not hoping that happens because I know some people do get better, after what—four and a half times? And you know, that's an average, but I couldn't even pick out eleven percent of people I know who have gotten better. Numbers can always be misleading, and this is probably one of those statistics where they have an asterisk at the bottom of the page. I just don't see it, though. Everybody I used to hang out with over here is either dead or in prison or in a nursing home.

"This town, though—it's ground zero. The pharmaceutical companies destroyed towns like ours. Just to give you some perspective on how bad Portsmouth was … I don't know many of the cops here now, but the old ones wanted to kill me. They would say, 'I hope I find you walking down an alley one night.' That's how bad it was." Chris shakes his head. "Little did they know, I was actually a coward. I didn't like confrontation."

"You mentioned that you don't steal anymore," I say. "What changed that?"

"Well, God played a big part," Chris says, but quickly adds, "It's hard for me to talk about that, though. I guess … I just don't want people to see me as a piece of crap. I don't care what people think who aren't relevant to my life. But those who are relevant, I do care. People are *starting* to understand that I don't steal things anymore, but they probably know I still get high. I don't know. I've created such a bad reputation for myself that it's probably a little late for me to try to get over it now.

"As a country, we just focus too much on the bad things someone's done. We punish them—for good reason because they should be punished—but we should build on their strengths more, too. We shouldn't just throw them in prison. We should find something they *can* do and build on that. It would probably help me if I had a wife. Someone to hold me accountable. I've never even had a girlfriend. I have a son, but it's not because I had a relationship with his mom. Biologically, he's not my son, though I'm proud of the fact he tells people I am. Those are the things that I need. I've spent the majority of my life in jail, though. I mean, I went to dive over the Second Street Bridge a few times, that's how bad it's been."

I'm surprised at how casually Chris mentions his attempted suicide. "What kept you from doing that?" I ask.

"I don't know." He breathes in deeply. "I was wanting to. But I dropped my bike and just took off running. I feel like it was God. I don't know that to be a fact, but something stopped me. I was bawling so bad I could hardly get up."

There's a long moment of silence between us. Finally, Chris goes on.

"My life fluctuates up and down for some reason. I'll do good for a little while, and then the lid pops off, and there's the guy we're all used to. I love this town, though. There ain't much to it, as you know, but it's my home and these are my people. I guess I just set my standards too high sometimes. I thought because I had all this experience teaching drug classes and stuff that these counseling centers were just gonna come running at me and beg me to work for them. But then reality hit me in the face when they said, 'Well, we'd like for you to have a year or two of sobriety under your belt.' For good reason. But that was a huge deal. That and my lack of healthy relationships has been a thorn in my side.

Chris knows some people who take Suboxone to manage their addiction. He admits that getting along with medication assistance is better than dying; however, his initial remarks about MAT were not entirely positive.

"The guy I work with is on the Suboxone program," he says. "The set-you-up-for-failure-on-a-different-drug program. That's what it really is. Suboxone is harder to come off of than heroin. I'm not sure how all this stuff came about. I tried to go volunteer my time at one of our local centers, so I could get my foot in the door to be a counselor, and I watched those guys go in and out and trade their dope for something else on the street. It's insane. Methadone is no different. Methadone and Suboxone are the only two substances the State will give people, and they are the only two things that are harder to get off of than heroin.

"Isn't it better for a person to be doing that than be out on the street, though?" I ask.

"Well, yeah, that's the flip side," Chris replies. "Take me, for instance. The heroin kept killing me. My buddy Narcan'd me thirteen times one night, all from one episode. I was pretty much dead. He was calling people on the phone to get them to bring their Narcan over. That guy literally saved my butt. I don't know if I even have the capability to ever be sober. I know that sounds crazy, and I don't *believe* that, but I do sometimes wonder. I try not to be the guy who sits around and criticizes everything because the fact of that matter is, we don't know a better way. There's no way of sitting down and really putting stakes in someone's life. You might be able to help a few people find a job or something, but as far as meaningful relationships go, you can't manufacture that. That stuff's gotta happen on its own. I would love to get married. I feel like the right woman would hold me accountable. Make me not want to die, you know? Just to wake up every morning next to someone I love ... that would be almost heaven."

I can't deny the truth behind either of Chris' positions. First, that no one else can give a person what they need to overcome addiction except themselves. Second, that human connection in the form of meaningful relationships is indispensable to give a person the strength and motivation they need to win that battle. More than once I found myself questioning this apparent contradiction in Chris' story. Only upon further reflection did I realize that there is no contradiction; the paradox itself is true.

Chris continues, "You know, criminologists and psychologists believe that once you've been incarcerated three times, the chances of you becoming a successful member of society are very slim. I appreciate those who want to find ways to help people, but as crazy as it sounds, folks just have to go through the school of hard knocks. I guess I could have graduated that school a little quicker myself. But it's like these kids out there running the street right now. Once that becomes the norm in their life, you can't change it. You just can't. I know nobody wants to hear that, and I don't want to say there's no hope at all ... "

Chris pauses, apparently redirecting his thoughts. "Like, they call me a 'life course persistent offender,' right? That's an LCP. Anyone who's had multiple prison terms. Petty criminals, basically. Two of the most well-known criminologists, Laub and Sampson, say that there's only three things that can change an LCP. One is military service. Two is the right partner or spouse. And three is ... "

Chris thinks long and hard but can't seem to remember the third option.

"Anyhow," he continues, "of the three things they say, two of them we're not even eligible for. Military service and"—it suddenly comes to him—"a good job. Right? Ok, so I've squandered multiple opportunities to have a good job. The right woman is not even on my radar, and I'm not on hers. And Portsmouth? There's nothing constructive here, especially for the kids. At some point they've just got to face the fact that the adults are gonna do what they do. I mean, I know that some people can get better, but most will not. The things that me and John wanted to do—that is literally an impossible task. It just is. If we really want to change our community, we have to start with the kids. The adults are gonna do what they do. They've reached a point in their life where that chaos is normal. They want it now. They crave it. And they should, because it gives them purpose. It would be stupid for me to sit here and suggest that the criminal lifestyle can't be exciting. So, in a very messed up sense, it gives people something to live for."

There is simple wisdom in Chris' insights. It is true, after all, that people crave meaning. Therefore, it makes sense to assume that if they can't find their purpose along conventional paths, such as a fulfilling career or relationship, they will walk down all kinds of dark alleyways to find it somewhere else. Toward the end of our conversation, Chris shifted the focus back to local recovery efforts. He seemed to do this every time it got too hard to keep talking about himself.

"You know, at some point there has to be boots on the ground," he explains. "Take John and the guys at RAW Addiction. John is the best man I know. I love that guy like my brother. But until they come up with resources to allow them to go into the streets, they're not gonna be able to make the impact they want to make. Like, go down here to the East End and ask anybody. They don't know what's going on in the recovery world. They've never heard about RAW Addiction. That's what I mean. They gotta find a way to put boots on the ground.

"It's like my mentor says. He's a professor at Belfast University. He uses the term 'generativity,'" which basically means you have to put something positive and meaningful back into the world. In order for me to do good myself, I have to be out there doing good in the world. If someone in the recovery community could organize something like this, it would have unprecedented results. I believe it would change the entire way treatment is administered. The biggest problem is, they don't want us addicts to be paraprofessionals. They don't want us to be working alongside psychologists because that would be a challenge to their status. But until that happens, things will continue to get worse.

"If I was out there right now with a role in an organization that helped individuals who suffer from the same things I do, that would be so huge for me, man. That would make me want to get up in the morning, drink a cup of coffee, and consider that my drug of the day. And that's not just me. Someone suggested to me once that this is just how *I* feel, and that not everyone else necessarily feels the same way. But I said, 'Go do something good for your mom or your dad and tell me the feeling you get from doing that isn't fulfilling.'

"I don't know, though. I had a few criminologists come and talk to me while I was in prison. After our visit, they said, 'You know, Chris, you're making me feel really stupid right now.' I said, 'Why?' They said, 'You just threw some common sense at me that I should have recognized a long time ago.' I just think anytime the solution can be extracted from the problem, that's the way to go. You can't staff a battered women's shelter with men. You can't put a straight guy in there to be an administrator in the LGBT community. It just doesn't work that way. So, why is it so hard for people to believe that an organized group of former criminals could be out there doing good things in the community? There's no program to replace that. No type of cognitive therapy could compare."

"What about Portsmouth?" I ask, seeking to bring the conversation to a close. "Some people think the tide has turned here and that things are starting to get better."

Chris laughs out loud. I tilt my head to the side and raise my eyebrows, anticipating his response.

"No," he says, sounding more certain of himself now than at any point in the conversation. "Absolutely not. Not even a little bit. Walk down Campbell Avenue at night. Go down by Jackson Street. They have a gang of kids down in some of the abandoned houses there. I was down there one day visiting a friend and they were sneaking around the building to try to jump us. I saw them coming and said, 'Listen here, little boy. I can't tell you what will happen if you do that, but you'd better not.' Luckily, we talked them down." Chris snorts. "Good thing, too, cause they'd have probably beat me up if we hadn't.

"It just seems like as time goes by, the age of juvenile delinquency continues to drop. There's little kids in Wayne Hills that are doing stuff I wasn't doing at thirteen or fourteen. It's insane. So, I guess to answer your question—and it hurts for me to say this, but it's a fact—sometimes you gotta just let the adults make their decisions and live with them, and then go and focus on the kids. It's why my hat goes off to people who are trying to help the adults, because they're just so unreachable. I wasn't reachable, at least. I may not even be now. I don't know.

"At the end of the day, I just want my family to be proud of me. That's something I haven't had a lot of, you know? I don't have many good achievements. I just want to be recognized as someone other than the guy who will steal your purse. I want to do things that allow me to build self-esteem because right now I'm beaten down. The craziest thing is that I know all this stuff. I know everything I'm doing wrong and what it would take for me to stop. But I don't do it."

"JESUS SAVES, BUT SO DOES NALOXONE."

T hroughout the process of writing *The Face of Addiction*, I would post a short blip about each person I interviewed on the project's Facebook page. Here's what I said about Chris Howard less than an hour after we spoke:

> Chris is at a place in his life where he has been written off by most of the people who know him, which is understandable considering the amount of harm he has caused over the years. Chris admits this fact without hesitation and offers no excuse for his actions. Nevertheless, the tears in his eyes spoke to me about the man he wants to be and the man he may yet become if he ever finds his way out of the darkness. If and when that day ever arrives, I suspect people are going to be surprised by the overwhelming amount of value that Chris has to offer the world.

When I wrote those words, I meant them. I would still hold this expectation if not for the fact that Chris died of an overdose on February 6, 2020, barely two months after he sat in my office and gave his interview. What he told me that day turned out to be true: "If I continue down this path, it's just a matter of time."

When I first heard the news of Chris' passing, it took me a moment to make the connection. I still had his cell phone number saved in my Word doc, so I could call him to review his story once the manuscript was complete. Then suddenly, he was just gone. Gone like the 130 other people who die from a drug overdose every day in America. If you add those numbers up over the course of a decade, it comes to a total determined by the CDC of 702,000 people who have fallen victim to the overdose epidemic from 1999–2017. Their names and faces live on now only in the memory of those who knew them and loved them as something more than just a drug addict.

Then there's Christine from chapter four. I've rarely met anyone whose enthusiasm for ending the stigma surrounding addiction was so palpable. I met Christine in the process of writing this book, and we stayed in touch following her interview. She ended up moving to my county, where I tried to help her connect with local friends and recovery allies. I even spent some time helping her write her own book, where she went into more detail about the hardships she had faced in life. The last time I spoke to her, she was busy preparing Christmas meals for families in need over the holiday season.

One month later, I received the news that Christine had died. I didn't know any of her family or close friends, so there was no one to contact. When I went to her Facebook page to try to determine what had happened, I found only three related posts, one from her niece and another from her daughter saying how much they missed her, and this haunting message from a friend: "I hope you are in a peaceful and forgiving place." Later, I was able to track down her daughter and offer my condolences. She affirmed what I already knew: Christine was "an amazing, inspiring, caring, and kindhearted woman."

As I think about Christine, Chris, and all the other people whose lives have been cut tragically short by this crisis, I feel a little overwhelmed. I've only known a few of them personally, but somebody knew all of them, and those are the folks who still live with the sorrow of their loved ones' passing. As I sit at my desk reflecting on the stories contained in this book, a lump forms in my throat. I stare at the computer screen and rack my brain for the right words to honor their memory. Chris Howard was just one person among many who found the painful complexity of his existence to be so unbearable that he would risk death in order to assuage or escape it. Yet, Chris was also a man who loved his mother and cared deeply about the abuse his family had suffered. He was intelligent and open to change. He desperately wanted to find better ways of helping guys like himself do what was right instead of what was wrong.

I wrote *The Face of Addiction* to help break down the cultural stigma surrounding people who use drugs that still pervades Appalachian culture. While being entirely honest about the destructive potential of substance abuse, I wanted to highlight the people themselves and those who loved them, whether in recovery or not, so that my readers could see them *as human beings*. Ending with Chris' story is somehow fitting.

Chris Howard wanted to be known as someone other than the guy who would steal your purse. While I understand this perspective will always be more difficult to take for the people whose purses Chris actually did steal, I still want you to see him as something more than a thief or drug addict. I want you to see beyond the tragic outcome of human brokenness to the value of humanity itself. I want you to see in Chris Howard, along with all the people who trusted me to tell their stories here, the face of addiction.

Although it is extremely difficult to sum up their representative experiences of loss, struggle, and recovery—all of which gets routinely lumped under the insanely impersonal category of the "opioid epidemic"—I hope to have done them some justice with these few simple words. If my literary odyssey in this field has taught me anything, it's that the roots of this crisis are inexplicably intertwined with the foundations of both human nature and human society. Thus, we can only do our best to respond with compassionate care.

As a person of faith, I've come to see many correlations between the concepts of sin and addiction that Christians, for instance, would do well to consider. When I hear the apostle Paul saying, "What I want to do, I don't do; what I don't want to do, I do" (Romans 7:19, New Living Translation), it's like I'm listening to a person with substance use disorder describe his or her daily inner battle. Didn't Chris end his interview by saying, "I know everything I'm doing wrong and what it would take for me to stop, but I don't do it"?

Where I come from, many people still see addiction as a moral failing when in reality it is a complex biopsychosocial issue. The biopsychosocial model is an interdisciplinary model that looks at the interconnection between biology, psychology, and socio-environmental factors. For me, that includes the "spiritual" aspect of life as well. Drug addiction involves personal choices, I'll grant that much, but so do certain forms of diabetes. Why should we classify one condition as a medical concern that is worthy of care and proper treatment while we look down our noses at the other as an individual moral failing? At any rate, even if a person's addiction began with some bad choices, once it reaches the level of chronic illness, it ceases to be a matter of simple choice.

At the same time, although substance use disorder can be accurately described as a chronic brain disease, it is far more than just that. Out beyond the religious view of addiction as a moral failing and the medical model of addiction as a chronic brain disease is a vast field that I am just beginning to explore. I hope you will join me in this quest for better understanding, because as you can see there are literally hundreds of thousands of lives hanging in the balance. Each one of those lives matters—to God, and I hope also to you. To that end, I want to leave you with some final thoughts on where to go from here.

There are three main ways to support recovery work: Prevention, treatment, and harm reduction. Prevention includes educating children about the risks and potential harms of drug use, yes. This is probably the first thing that comes to mind for most people when the question of prevention comes up. But as a standalone option, this kind of "education" is woefully inadequate. If the D.A.R.E. program of the 1980's taught us anything, it's that "Just Say No" is not an effective approach to keep most kids from using drugs. My apologies to Nancy Reagan.

Prevention should also include teaching children the practice of mindfulness. Social emotional learning programs like the one being developed in the Minford, OH school system, for instance, are just beginning to scratch the surface of what is possible in terms of genuine substance abuse prevention. Kendra Rase Cram is the first full-time Social Emotional Learning (SEL) teacher in the state of Ohio. She praises her school's administration for having the vision to become proactive in providing preventative tools for the children in their care.

"My SEL work has exploded beyond expectation," Kendra says. "It is the first SEL program that offers direct instruction to every child as a required class in the state of Ohio. The way the program works is that each student comes for forty-five minutes a week from Kindergarten through fifth grade. This equals *234 hours of conversation* that kids have had about drugs, managing emotions, self-regulation, conflict resolution, etc. before they even enter 6th grade … We believe these 'soft skills' are the most difficult to master and are the ones we humans get the least instruction on" (Cram, 2020).

Young adults who have been trained in various coping skills are less likely to turn to drugs when they encounter stressful situations. And when they do turn to substance use, or when they live with parents and grandparents who do, they need to be given a safe space in which to process their emotions and experiences. Ask Jocelyn Cooper, the spokesperson for Directly Affected, another homegrown nonprofit organization that provides peer recovery support in Scioto County, what a difference that makes. Directly Affected meets once a week to provide peer-led support for teenagers who have been impacted by the opioid epidemic. Community sponsors provide free meals for all the youth who attend.

"I just want other kids to get the help they need," Jocelyn says. "I wish that I had something like this a couple years ago. And I'm sure there's a lot of adults who have already gone down the wrong path who wish they had this when they were teenagers, too" (Directly Affected, 2020).

Then there's the foster care system. For every success story you hear from the hardworking parents, judges, respite caregivers, Court Appointed Special Advocates (CASA), and social workers, all of whom are doing their best to provide for the needs of nearly 450,000 children currently awaiting their "forever home" across the United States (U.S. Department of Health and Human Services, 2018), there must be five horror stories of kids being abused, neglected, or simply aging out of the system to enter life in the streets on their own. My home state of Ohio saw a nine percent increase in children in foster care from 2013 to 2017 (NACAC, 2018). There's just no other way to put it: we have to do better.

That's not all, of course, not by a long shot. There are other ways, some less obvious and more complex, in which we set our children up for failure across the western world. Being the "big picture" thinker that I am, I'm partial to such theories as the one advanced by Bruce Alexander, who argues that addiction is increasing across the world in such sharp degree due to the general fragmentation of human society. In his 2010 book, *The Globalization of Addiction: A Study in Poverty of the Spirit*, he writes,

> "Addictive problems in one's personal world need not provoke despair because they are not manifestations of mental illness or malice, but of a struggle to survive. Nor are they abnormal. Many, perhaps most, of our compatriots in the new global civilization live with addictive dynamics of some degree. Like us, they are neither diseased nor evil at heart. Like us, they find themselves unable to endure the lack of psychosocial integration without becoming, at times, overwhelmingly involved with habits that partially substitute for it. Like us, they sometimes act badly, wastefully, recklessly, but without evil intent. There is no reason for despair over dislocation either, because it does not grow from a lack of personal worth or human appeal, but from a fragmented society" (p. 340)

In other words, there is far more to drug prevention than normally meets the eye. And while many of our politicians are willing, at least for the moment, to throw big money at America's collective effort to "combat" the opioid crisis, these are issues that very few of them are willing to honestly and thoroughly engage. For the purpose of keeping this conclusion as actionable as possible, though, I will try to keep my head out of the ideological clouds and focus on those few things that are more likely to be within your personal reach to either do or support.

Treatment deals with the opposite end of the spectrum, where the concern lies primarily with people who have already turned to the misuse of substances as a way to manage their hectic lives, cope with unresolved pain, or [insert your own reason here]. In the words of the Big Book, these are the folks whose lives have admittedly "become unmanageable" (Anonymous, 2001). Step one in any case is to admit that you have a problem. Where you go from there is a matter of which program you follow.

In central Appalachia, the AA and NA tradition still ranks atop the field in most people's approach to treatment. You'll never find me disparaging any 12-step program, if only because they bear such a striking resemblance to the faith tradition in which I was raised. I tend to agree with the principle that "it works if you work it," at least in theory (Anonymous, 2001). Yet, at the same time, I like to follow the evidence, and the numbers do not suggest a high success rate for 12-step programs when taken alone. There is a growing body of evidence, however, for the effectiveness of medication-assisted treatment (MAT). Not only does MAT seem to increase one's chances for long-term recovery, but it also reduces a lot of potential harm along the way. Federally approved medications for drug treatment assistance include substances like Methadone, Suboxone, and Vivitrol.

Absorbing all the information related to recovery can be difficult for people who are new to the field, so I want to be careful not to overwhelm you with options and statistics. Becoming a member of your local coalition would be a great way to find out what services are available in your area. Most of the public health workers and addiction and mental health service providers you'll meet are working in this field for all the right reasons, and they love to share information that will help folks get the assistance they need. You can always check with your local Alcohol Drug Addiction Mental Health Services (ADAMHS) board or public health director for a list of available options.

Finally, in between prevention and treatment is harm reduction. While there is no universally accepted definition of harm reduction, according to Harm Reduction International it generally refers to "policies, programs and practices that aim to minimize negative health, social and legal impacts associated with drug use, drug policies and drug laws" (Harm Reduction International, n.d.). The guiding philosophical light behind harm reduction is that *every person's life is valuable* regardless of the mess they might be in. Operating from this basic principle, harm reductionists will distribute and carry the opioid overdose reversal drug naloxone, receive training on how to recognize and respond to an overdose, and advocate for more humane drug policies at the local, state, and federal levels. Some of them even write books to get people to see the humanity in their friends and family members who use drugs.

For people of faith, harm reduction is a pro-life issue. You can't take seriously the words of Jesus in Matthew 25:40, that whatever you've done to the "least of" his brothers and sisters—in other words, the most vulnerable members of society—you've done also to him, and yet still argue that overdose victims should be left to die in the streets. It just doesn't work that way. Some of my strongest personal sentiments lie here, so I think this is a good place to end our conversation.

As much as I hate to admit it, American culture is still rife with stigma against people who suffer with substance use disorder. Did they make the initial choice to use drugs? Sure, but addiction is a nasty beast. It changes you in ways you don't see coming and brings you into bondage. Anyone who has suffered through it will tell you. There's even a lot of science behind this assertion if you care to do your homework.

None of this changes the value of a human being, though, regardless of how far gone a person might seem to be. As long as they are still breathing, there is hope for recovery. Redemption knows no limits. This is why harm reduction should be a given for people of faith and goodwill. Yes, Jesus saves—but so does naloxone. Keeping people alive in the hope that they will get the help they need is one of the best ways to practice your faith.

So, go into all the world and preach the Gospel, and while you do, make sure you educate and inform them about this crisis. People need to know what's happening here in southern Ohio and around the world. Our brothers and sisters are dying before their time, and not only the faith community but society as a whole needs to step up its game.

I've never experienced substance use disorder, so when people ask me why I care about the opioid epidemic, I think of all the friends and family we have lost to the abyss of addiction. They deserve my time and attention, and they deserve yours, too. Furthermore, I think about those two guys from the preface of this book who helped me get through my own personal crisis. My life wouldn't be the same without them, and I believe this potentially holds true for everybody who is still fighting their way to recovery.

In other words, there's not a single person out there with a needle in their arm right now whose life doesn't matter. That man living in the abandoned house belongs in our community. The single mom who's fresh out of rehab trying to find a job deserves a second chance. Their lives are bursting with potential. We don't even know what treasures they possess. This is what my experience has taught me, and if it's your thing, this is also what the Gospel of Jesus Christ declares. So, deal with it and get on board.

"NOT EVERY STORY HAS A HAPPY ENDING ... BUT THE DISCOVERIES OF SCIENCE, THE TEACHINGS OF THE HEART, AND THE REVELATIONS OF THE SOUL ALL ASSURE US THAT NO HUMAN BEING IS EVER BEYOND REDEMPTION. THE POSSIBILITY OF RENEWAL EXISTS SO LONG AS LIFE EXISTS. HOW TO SUPPORT THAT POSSIBILITY IN OTHERS AND OURSELVES IS THE ULTIMATE QUESTION."

– **Dr. Gabor Maté**
In the Realm of Hungry Ghosts: Close Encounters with Addiction

REFERENCES

1. Alexander, B. (2010). *The Globalization of Addiction: A Study in Poverty of the Spirit.* Oxford: Oxford University Press.

2. Anonymous. (2001). *Alcoholics Anonymous: The Big Book.*

3. Borger, J. (2001). "Hillbilly Heroin: The Painkiller Abuse Wrecking Lives in West Virginia." *The Guardian.* Retrieved from https://www.theguardian.com/world/2001/jun/25/usa.julianborger

4. Brown, B. (2007). *I Thought It Was Just Me: Women Reclaiming Power and Courage In A Culture of Shame.* New York: Gotham Books.

5. Centers for Disease Control and Prevention (CDC). (n.d.). *Opiod Overdose.* Retrieved from https://www.cdc.gov/drugoverdose/data/prescribing/overview.html

6. Centers for Disease Control and Prevention (CDC). (2018). *Drug Overdose Death Rates.* Retrieved from https://www.cdc.gov/drugoverdose/data/statedeaths/drug-overdose-death-2018.html

7. Cohen G. (2001). The 'Poor Man's Heroin'. An Ohio Surgeon Helps Feed A Growing Addiction To OxyContin. *U.S. News & World Report, 130*(6), 27.

8. Cram, K. R. (personal communication, May 39, 2020) stated her involvement in Socio-Emotional Learning.

9. Directly Affected. (c.a. 2020). In *Facebook* [Group page]. Retrieved June 12, 2020, from https://www.facebook.com/Directly-Affected-100138551471303

10. Drug Enforcement Agency. (n.d.) *Narcotics (Opioids).* Retrieved from https://www.dea.gov/taxonomy/term/331

11. Hari, J. (2015). *Everything You Think You Know About Addiction Is Wrong.* [Video File] https://www.ted.com/talks/johann_hari_everything_you_think_you_know_about_addiction_is_wrong/up-next?language=en

12. Harm Reduction International. (n.d.) "What Is Harm Reduction?" Retrieved from https://www.hri.global/what-is-harm-reduction#:~:text=Harm%20reduc-tion%20refers%20to%20policies,drug%20policies%20and%20drug%20 laws.

13. Maté, G. (2010). *In the Realm of Hungry Ghosts: Close Encounters With Addiction.* Berkley: North Atlantic Books.

14. Martin, K. U.S. Drug Enforcement Agency. *(2011).* "Jury Convicts Physician For Illegally Prescribing Pills That Led To Deaths of Four People." Retrieved from https://www.dea.gov/press-releases/2011/05/10/jury-convicts-physician-illegally-prescribing-pills-led-deaths-four

15. North American Council on Adoptable Children (NACAC). (2018). "Foster Care Numbers Up Fifth Straight Year." Retrieved from https://www.nacac.org/2019/01/18/foster-care-numbers-up-for-fifth-straight-year/

16. Nutt, A. (2016). *Becoming Nicole: The Transformation of An American Family.* New York: Random House.

17. Ohio Department of Health. (2018). *2018 Ohio Drug Overdose Data: Geographic Summary.* Retrieved from: https://odh.ohio.gov/wps/wcm/connect/gov/85194270-e6a7-49c4-aacb-bcfa8f62c558/2018_Ohio+Drug+Overdose_Geographic+Summary.pdf?MOD=AJPERES&CONVERT_TO=url&CACHEID=ROOTWORKSPACE.Z18_M1HGGIK0N0JO00QO9DDDDM3000-85194270-e6a7-49c4-aacb-bcfa8f62c558-n1ERQ5G

18. Sony Pictures Home Entertainment (Firm). (2009). *Breaking Bad: The Complete First Season.* Culver City, Calif: Sony Pictures Home Entertainment.

19. Stevenson, B. (2014). *Just Mercy.* New York: Random House.

20. Stigma. (n.d.). In *Merriam-Webster.com Dictionary.* Retrieved from https://www.merriam-webster.com/dictionary/stigma

21. U.S. Centers for Disease Control and Prevention. "America's Drug Overdose Epidemics: Data To Action." Retrieved January 2, 2020, from https://www.cdc.gov/injury/features/prescription-drug-overdose/index.html

22. U.S. Department of Health and Human Services. (2000, April 1). "Report To The President: Prescription Drug Coverage, Spending, Utilization, and Prices." Office of the Assistant Secretary for Planning and Evaluation. Retrieved from https://aspe.hhs.gov/report/

report-president-prescription-drug-coverage-spending-utilization-and-prices/
ims-health-data

23. U.S. Department of Health and Human Services. (2018). "The AFCARS
Report: Preliminary Fy 2017 Estimates As of August 10, 2018" (25). Retrieved
from https://www.acf.hhs.gov/cb/resource/afcars-report-25

24. U.S. Drug Enforcement Administration. "Narcotics (Opioids)." Retrieved
November 23, 2019, from https://www.dea.gov/taxonomy/term/331

Many voices. One message.

Quoir is a boutique publisher
with a singular message: *Christ is all.*
Venture beyond your boundaries to discover Christ
in ways you never thought possible.

For more information, please visit
www.quoir.com

CPSIA information can be obtained
at www.ICGtesting.com
Printed in the USA
LVHW050031070921
697098LV00002B/109